READ WELL

Life as an Ant

Teacher's Guide

Unit 5

ow says /ōōō/
Voiced
(Long)

open syllable /ō/
as in open and
moment

means full of
as in colorful

Note: See New and Important Objectives on page 2 for a complete list of skills taught and reviewed.

Critical Foundations in Primary Reading

Marilyn Sprick, Ann Watanabe, Karen Akiyama-Paik, and Shelley V. Jones

Sopris West®
EDUCATIONAL SERVICES

A Cambium Learning® Company

BOSTON, MA • LONGMONT, CO

ISBN 13-digit: 978-1-60218-528-9
ISBN 10-digit: 1-60218-528-X

13 12 11 10 09 08   1 2 3 4 5 6

166887

Table of Contents
Unit 5
Life as an Ant

End of the Unit

Letter Sounds and Combinations

Cumulative Review of *Read Well 1* Sounds and Combinations (Ss, Ee, ee, Mm, Aa, Dd, th, Nn, Tt, Ww, Ii, Th, Hh, Cc, Rr, ea, sh, Sh, Kk, -ck, oo, ar, wh, Wh, ĕ, -y as in fly, Ll, Oo, Bb, all, Gg, Ff, Uu, er, oo as in book, Yy, a schwa, Pp, ay, Vv, Qq, Jj, Xx, or, Zz, a_e, -y as in baby, i_e, ou, ow as in cow, ch, Ch, ai, igh, o_e, ir) and:

Unit 2	Unit 3		Unit 5	Unit 6
aw /aw/ **Paw** Voiced	**ew** /o͞o/ **Crew** Voiced	**ue** /o͞o/ **Blue** Voiced	**u_e** /o͞o/ **Flute** Bossy E Voiced	**ow** /ō͞ō/ **Snow** Voiced (Long)	**ge** /j/ **Page** Voiced

Unit 6	Unit 7		Unit 8		Unit 10
-dge /j/ **Badge** Voiced	**ci** /sss/ **Circle** Unvoiced	**ce** /sss/ **Center** Unvoiced	**kn** /nnn/ **Knee** Voiced	**ph** /fff/ **Phone** Unvoiced	**oa** /ō͞ō/ **Boat** Voiced (Long)

Unit 11		Unit 12		Unit 13
oi /oi/ **Point** Voiced	**ea** /ĕĕĕ/ **Bread** Voiced (Short)	**gi** /j/ **Giraffe** Voiced	**au** /au/ **Astronaut** Voiced	**oy** /oy/ **Boy** Voiced

Affixes (including morphographs—affixes taught with meaning) and Open Syllables

Cumulative Review of *Read Well 1* Affixes (-ed, -en, -es, -ing, -ly, -s, -y, -tion) and:

Unit 2	Unit 3		Unit 5		Unit 6
re- **Means again** as in reread	**un-** **Means not** as in unhappy	**ex-** as in excited	**o** Open syllable /ō/ as in open and moment	**-ful** **Means full of** as in colorful	**bi-** **Means two** as in bicycle

Unit 7	Unit 8	Unit 11	Unit 12	Unit 13	
de- as in detective	**-able** as in comfortable	**i** Open syllable /ī/ as in silence and pilot	**be-** as in before	**-ous** as in enormous	**dis-** as in discover

Unit 14		Unit 15		Unit 16	
-al as in animal	**-ible** as in flexible	**-or** **Means one who** as in actor	**-ment** as in apartment	**-ic** as in scientific	**pre-** **Means before** as in preview

Unit 17		Unit 18		Unit 19	
-ity as in activity	**-sion** as in permission	**-ness** as in fairness	**-less** **Means without** as in helpless	**in-** as in insert	**im-** **Means not** as in impossible

Introduction
Life as an Ant

Story Notes

Unit 5 continues the theme of communities. In this unit, students learn how ants live and work together.

Ant Communities: Did you know that ants have been around since the time of the dinosaurs? Did you know their nests have garbage dumps? Your students will have fun learning fascinating facts about these little creatures.

An Ant With Ideas: After learning how ants live and work together, it isn't hard to imagine an ant with ideas. Antonia Ant uses creativity and ingenuity to solve problems in her bustling community.

Recommended Read Alouds

The *Read Well 2* suggested Read Aloud stories enhance small group instruction—providing opportunities to further build background knowledge and vocabulary.

> **CAUTION**
> **(Reminder)**
> Do not read the Read Aloud recommendations during small group instruction. Reserve this time for students to read.

The Life and Times of the Ant by Charles Micucci
Nonfiction • Expository

We see small ants all the time, but how much do we know about them? Select from a broad menu of topics to capture children's interest—where ants live, how they communicate, and how they help recycle the rain forest. After hearing Micucci's book, your students may conclude that ants are indeed "Masters of the Earth."

Read Well Connections
Micucci's nonfiction selection expands on information students read in Unit 5. For example, students learn that all ants have antennas. In *The Life and Times of an Ant*, students learn that antennas have more than a thousand hairs that sense vibrations.

NOTE FROM THE AUTHORS

KNOWLEDGE IS POWER

Unit 5 is *Read Well 2's* first science unit. Students learn to make connections, build on prior knowledge, preview text, and locate information. Comprehension work prepares students for more complex report writing in Unit 14. Your students will take pride in their ability to read this nonfiction selection. Show your enthusiasm by describing their accomplishments:

Wow, you can tell your parents what makes an ant an insect. Now you know what goes on in an anthill. Next time you see one, you will know what is happening under the dirt.

New and Important Objectives
A Research-Based Reading Program

Phonemic Awareness
Phonics
Fluency
Vocabulary
Comprehension

Phonological and Phonemic Awareness

Blending; Rhyming; Onset and Rime; Counting Syllables

Phonics

Cumulative Letter Sounds and Combinations

Review • Ss, Ee, ee, Mm, Aa, Dd, th, Nn, Tt, Ww, Ii, Th, Hh, Cc, Rr, ea, sh, Sh, Kk, -ck, oo, ar, wh, Wh, ĕ, -y (as in fly), Ll, Oo, Bb, all, Gg, Ff, Uu, er, oo (as in book), Yy, a (schwa), Pp, ay, Vv, Qq, Jj, Xx, or, Zz, a_e, -y (as in baby), i_e, ou, ow (as in cow), ch, Ch, ai, igh, o_e, ir, aw, ew, ue, u_e

Cumulative Affixes and Morphographs

Review • -ed, -en, -er, -es, -est, -ing, -ly, -s, -y, -tion, re-, un-, ex-

☆ New Letter Sounds and Combinations, Affixes, and Morphographs

ow (as in snow) • blow, flow, follow, low, slowed, snow

-ful • cheerful, helpful, painful, respectful, restful, useful

o (as in open and moment) • frozen, motion

☆ New Proper Nouns

Antonia, Antonia's

☆ New Contractions

we've

☆ New Abbreviations

T. rex

2

Phonics (continued)

⭐ **New Pattern Words**

bathe, bite, blues, chest, chunks, claw, drag, dragging, fed, grain, guard, line, march, marched, minds, molt, molting, path, proud, queen's, roll, rolled, roof, shin, skin, skinny, spin, spins, stray, swirl, swirled, taste, third, trail, wave, wheels, zag, zagged, zig, zigged, zone

  ***Known Pattern Words With Affixes** • cans, cried, drinking, finding, finds, jobs, keeping, kinds, listed, makes, painting, rooms, smelly, strongest, time's, turns, waiter, unlit, unused, using

⭐ **New Compound and Hyphenated Words**

anthill, butterflies, cleanup, leftover, matchbox, mouth-watering, outside, sunshine

⭐ **Other New Multisyllabic Words**

abdomen, adults, alarm, anatomy, antenna, antennas, attack, attacked, beside, bodies, body, caterpillar, cocoon, cocoons, collapse, collapsing, colonies, colony, communities, community, construct, construction, dawdle, enemies, enemy, expect, extra, female, females, hospital, invention, larvas, liquids, marble, marbles, markers, nurseries, nursery, several, survive, survivors, temperature, thorax, tunnel, underneath, waggle, waggled, winter

  ***Known Multisyllabic Words With Affixes** • adults, amazingly, buttons, returns, wiggled

⭐ **New Tricky Words**

above, accident, chamber, chambers, change, changed, cycle, danger, dead, duty, entrance, imagination, label, metamorphosis, pupas, service, since, stage, stages, stomachs, storage, swarm, tiny, treasure, treasures, warm, warn, weight, worms

  ***Known Tricky Words With Affixes** • babies, dinosaurs, fourth, millions, pushed, workers

Fluency

Accuracy, Expression, Phrasing, Rate

Vocabulary

New • collapse, colony, community, dawdle, except, imagination, impressed, life cycle, metamorphosis, molt, protect, survive, treasure

Review • habitat

Reviewed in Context • amazing, inventor, sturdy, treasure

3

Comprehension

Unit Genres

Nonfiction • Expository
Fiction • Imaginative

Comprehension Processes

Build Knowledge: Factual, Procedural, Conceptual

Day	1	2	3	4	5	6
Remember						
Defining	S	S				C
Identifying (recalling)	S,C	E,S,C	S,C	S,C	S,C	S,C
Using	S	S				
Understand						
Defining (in your own words)	S	S		S		
Describing	S	S	S	S,C	S,C	S,C
Explaining (rephrasing)	S,C	E,S	C	S	S,C	S
Illustrating		C	C	C		
Sequencing				C	C	
Summarizing		E,S			C	
Using	S	E,S,C	S,C	S,C	S,C	S
Visualizing					S,C	
Apply						
Demonstrating						
Explaining (unstated)	S		C	S	S	C
Illustrating					C	
Inferring	S,C	S		S	S	C
Making Connections (relating)	S		S	S		
Predicting				S	S	
Using	S,C	S,C		S,C	S	
Analyze						
Classifying	S			S		
Comparing/Contrasting						
Distinguishing Cause/Effect						
Drawing Conclusions	C			S,C		
Inferring				C		S
Evaluate						
Making Judgments				S	S	S
Responding (personal)	S		C			
Create						
Generating Ideas			C			

E = Exercise, S = Storybook, C = Comprehension & Skill

Comprehension (continued)

Skills and Strategies

Day	1	2	3	4	5	6
Priming Background Knowledge	S	E,S		S		
Setting a Purpose for Reading	S			S		
Answering Questions	S	S	S	S	S	S
Asking Questions	S	S	S			
Visualizing						
Comprehension Monitoring/Fix Ups						
Does it Make Sense?	C	C		C	C	
Looking Back	C	E,C	C	C	C	
Restating						
Summarizing						
Main Idea	C					
Retelling					C	
Supporting Details						
Understanding Text Structure						
Title, Author, Illustrator	S	E,S	S	S		
Fact or Fiction	S					
Genre (Classifying)	S			S		
Narrative						
Setting				C	C	
Main Character/Traits (Characterization)				S,C	C	C
Goal				C	S,C	C
Problem/Solution				S	S	C
Action/Events/Sequence					C	S
Outcome/Conclusion				C	C	
Lesson/Author's Message						
Expository						
Subject/Topic	C					
Heading	S	S	S			
Supporting Details (Facts/Information)	S,C	E,S	S,C			
Main Idea	C					
Using Graphic Organizers						
Chart			C			
Diagram (labeling)	C		C			
Hierarchy (topic/detail)						
K-W-L	S	S	S			
Map (locating, labeling)						
Matrix (compare/contrast)						
Sequence (linear, cycle, cause and effect)		S,C		C		
Story Map					C	
Web				C	C	

E = Exercise, S = Storybook, C = Comprehension & Skill

Comprehension *(continued)*

Study Skills

Day	1	2	3	4	5	6
Alphabetical Order						
Following Directions	C					
Locating Information		E,S				
Note Taking						
Previewing			S			
Reviewing		S		S	S	
Test Taking						C
Using Glossary						
Using Table of Contents	S			S		
Viewing		S	S	S		
Verifying	S	S	S			

Writing in Response to Reading

Day	1	2	3	4	5	6
Sentence Completion	C	C	C		C	C
Making Lists		C				
Sentence Writing	C	C	C		C	C
Story Retell/Summary					C	
Fact Summary		E	C			
Paragraph Writing						
Report Writing						
Open-Ended Response			C			
Creative Writing						

Writing Traits

(Addressed within the context of Writing in Response to Reading)

Day	1	2	3	4	5	6
Ideas and Content						
Elaborating/Generating						
Organization						
Introduction					C	
Topic Sentence						
Supporting Details						
Sequencing				C	C	
Word Choice						
Sophisticated Words (Tier 2 and 3)						
Conventions						
Capital	C	C	C		C	C
Ending Punctuation	C	C	C		C	C
Other (commas, quotation marks)						
Presentation						
Handwriting	C	C	C	C	C	C
Neatness	C	C	C	C	C	C

E = Exercise, S = Storybook, C = Comprehension & Skill

Daily Lesson Planning

LESSON PLAN FORMAT

Teacher-Directed 45 Minutes		Independent Teacher-Directed, as needed
Lesson Part 1 (Phonological Awareness, Phonics, Fluency, Comprehension) 15–20 Minutes	**Lesson Part 2** (Vocabulary, Fluency, Comprehension) 20–25 Minutes	**Lesson Part 3** (Vocabulary, Fluency, Comprehension) 15–20 Minutes
• Exercises	• Unit and/or Story Opener • Vocabulary • Interactive Story Reading • Short Passage Practice Timed Readings	• Story Reading With Partner or Whisper Reading • Comprehension and Skill Activities

HOMEWORK

Read Well 2 Homework (blackline masters of new *Read Well 2* passages) provides an opportunity for children to celebrate accomplishments with parents. Homework should be sent home on routine days.

ORAL READING FLUENCY ASSESSMENT

Upon completion of this unit, assess each student and proceed to Unit 6, as appropriate.

WRITTEN ASSESSMENT

Upon completion of this unit, students will be administered a Written Assessment that can be found on page 80 in the student's *Activity Book 1*.

Note: See Making Decisions for additional assessment information.

DIFFERENTIATED LESSON PLANS

The differentiated lesson plans illustrate how materials can be used for students with various learning needs. As you set up your unit plan, always include *Read Well 2* Exercises and Story Reading on a daily basis. Unit 5 includes 6-, 8-, 9-, 10-, and 11-Day Plans.

Plans	For groups that:
6-DAY	Complete Oral Reading Fluency Assessments with Passes and Strong Passes
8-DAY	Complete Oral Reading Fluency Assessments with Passes and require teacher-guided assistance with Story Reading and Comprehension and Skill Work
9-, 10-, or 11-DAY	Have difficulty passing the unit Oral Reading Fluency Assessments

6-DAY PLAN

Day 1

Teacher-Directed
- Exercise 1
- Unit and Story Opener: Life as an Ant, Ant Communities
- K-W-L (modified)
- Vocabulary, Ch. 1, 2
- Ant Communities, Ch. 1
- Guide practice, as needed, on Comp & Skill 1, 2

Independent Work
- On Your Own: Partner or Whisper Read, Ant Communities, Ch. 2
- Comp & Skill Activities 1, 2

Homework
- Homework Passage 1

Day 2

Teacher-Directed
- Exercise 2a
- Exercise 2b: Focus Lesson
- Vocabulary, Ch. 3, 4
- Ant Communities, Ch. 3
- Guide practice, as needed, on Comp & Skill 3, 4

Independent Work
- Repeated Reading: Partner or Whisper Read, Ant Communities, Ch. 3
- Comp & Skill Activities 3, 4

Homework
- Homework Passage 2

Day 3

Teacher-Directed
- Exercise 3
- Ant Communities, Ch. 4
- K-W-L (modified)
- Guide practice, as needed, on Comp & Skill 5a, 5b

Independent Work
- Repeated Reading: Partner or Whisper Read, Ant Communities, Ch. 4
- Comp & Skill Activities 5a, 5b

Homework
- Homework Passage 3

Day 4

Teacher-Directed
- Story Opener: An Ant With Ideas
- Exercise 4
- Vocabulary, Ch. 1–3
- An Ant With Ideas, Ch. 1
- Guide practice, as needed, on Comp & Skill 6, 7

Independent Work
- On Your Own: Partner or Whisper Read, An Ant With Ideas, Ch. 2
- Comp & Skill Activities 6, 7

Homework
- Homework Passage 4

Day 5

Teacher-Directed
- Exercise 5
- An Ant With Ideas, Ch. 3
- Guide practice, as needed, on Comp & Skill 8, 9a, 9b

Independent Work
- Repeated Reading: Partner or Whisper Read, An Ant With Ideas, Ch. 3
- Comp & Skill Activities 8, 9a, 9b

Homework
- Homework Passage 5

Day 6

Teacher-Directed
- Exercise 6
- Fluency, The Lost Treasure

Independent Work
- Repeated Reading: Partner or Whisper Read, The Lost Treasure
- Written Assessment
- Oral Reading Fluency Assessment*

Homework
- Homework Passage 6

Note: Unit 5 features an extra Just for Fun Comp & Skill activity, located after Activity 7. This page can be used any time after "An Ant With Ideas," Chapter 2. The Just for Fun activity allows the related activities, story map and written retell, to be located side by side in the Activity Book.

*The Oral Reading Fluency Assessments are individually administered by the teacher while students are working on their Written Assessments.

Day 1

Teacher-Directed
- Exercise 1
- Unit and Story Opener: Life as an Ant, Ant Communities
- K-W-L modified
- Vocabulary, Ch. 1, 2
- Ant Communities, Ch. 1
- Guide practice, as needed, on Comp & Skill 1

Independent Work
- Repeated Reading: Partner or Whisper Read, Ant Communities, Ch. 1
- Comp & Skill Activity 1

Homework
- Homework Passage 1

Day 2

Teacher-Directed
- Review Exercise 1
- Review Vocabulary, Ch. 1, 2
- Ant Communities, Ch. 2
- Guide practice, as needed, on Comp & Skill 2

Independent Work
- Repeated Reading: Partner or Whisper Read, Ant Communities, Ch. 2
- Comp & Skill Activity 2

Homework
- Teacher's Choice

Day 3

Teacher-Directed
- Exercise 2a
- Exercise 2b: Focus Lesson
- Vocabulary, Ch. 3, 4
- Ant Communities, Ch. 3
- Guide practice, as needed, on Comp & Skill 3, 4

Independent Work
- Repeated Reading: Partner or Whisper Read, Ant Communities, Ch. 3
- Comp & Skill Activities 3, 4

Homework
- Homework Passage 2

Day 4

Teacher-Directed
- Exercise 3
- Review Vocabulary, Ch. 3, 4
- Ant Communities, Ch. 4
- Guide practice, as needed, on Comp & Skill 5a, 5b

Independent Work
- Repeated Reading: Partner or Whisper Read, Ant Communities, Ch. 4
- Comp & Skill Activities 5a, 5b

Homework
- Homework Passage 3

Day 5

Teacher-Directed
- Exercise 4
- Story Opener: An Ant With Ideas
- Vocabulary, Ch. 1–3
- An Ant With Ideas, Ch. 1
- Guide practice, as needed, on Comp & Skill 6

Independent Work
- Repeated Reading: Partner or Whisper Read, An Ant With Ideas, Ch. 1
- Comp & Skill Activity 6

Homework
- Homework Passage 4

Day 6

Teacher-Directed
- Review Exercise 4
- Review Vocabulary, Ch. 1–3
- An Ant With Ideas, Ch. 2
- Guide practice, as needed, on Comp & Skill 7

Independent Work
- Repeated Reading: Partner or Whisper Read, An Ant With Ideas, Ch. 2
- Comp & Skill Activity 7

Homework
- Comp & Skill Activity 4 (Passage Fluency)

Day 7

Teacher-Directed
- Exercise 5
- Review Vocabulary, Ch. 1–3
- An Ant With Ideas, Ch. 3
- Guide practice, as needed, on Comp & Skill 8, 9a, 9b

Independent Work
- Repeated Reading: Partner or Whisper Read, An Ant With Ideas, Ch. 3
- Comp & Skill Activities 8, 9a, 9b

Homework
- Homework Passage 5

Day 8

Teacher-Directed
- Exercise 6
- Fluency, The Lost Treasure

Independent Work
- Repeated Reading: Partner or Whisper Read, The Lost Treasure
- Oral Reading Fluency Assessment*
- Written Assessment

Homework
- Homework Passage 6

Day 9 Extra Practice 1

Teacher-Directed
- Decoding Practice
- Fluency Passage

Independent Work
- Activity and Word Fluency A

Homework
- Fluency Passage

Day 10 Extra Practice 2

Teacher-Directed
- Decoding Practice
- Fluency Passage

Independent Work
- Activity and Word Fluency B

Homework
- Fluency Passage

Day 11 Extra Practice 3

Teacher-Directed
- Decoding Practice
- Fluency Passage

Independent Work
- Activity and Word Fluency A or B
- Oral Reading Fluency Assessment*

Homework
- Fluency Passage

Materials and Materials Preparation

Core Lessons

Teacher Materials

READ WELL 2 MATERIALS

- Unit 5 Teacher's Guide
- Sound Cards
- Unit 5 Oral Reading Fluency Assessment found on page 86
- Group Assessment Record found in the *Assessment Manual*

SCHOOL SUPPLIES

Stopwatch or watch with a second hand

Student Materials

READ WELL 2 MATERIALS (for each student)

- *Communities* storybook
- *Exercise Book 1*
- *Activity Book 1* or copies of Unit 5 Comprehension and Skill Work
- Unit 5 Written Assessment found in *Activity Book 1*, page 80, and on the blackline master CD
- Unit 5 Certificate of Achievement/Goal Setting (BLM, page 87)
- Unit 5 Homework (blackline masters)
  See *Getting Started* for suggested homework routines.

SCHOOL SUPPLIES

Pencils, colors (optional—markers, crayons, or colored pencils)

> Make one copy per student of each blackline master, as appropriate for the group.
>
> *Note:* For new or difficult Comprehension and Skill Activities, make overhead transparencies from the blackline masters. Use the transparencies to demonstrate and guide practice.

> **FOCUS LESSONS**
> For Exercise 2b (Focus Lesson), make overhead transparencies from the blackline masters, write on transparencies placed over the pages, or use paper copies to demonstrate how to complete the lessons.

Extra Practice Lessons

> **CAUTION**
> Use these lessons only if needed. Students who need Extra Practice may benefit from one, two, or three lessons.

Student Materials

READ WELL 2 MATERIALS (for each student, as needed)

See Extra Practice blackline masters located on the CD.

- Unit 5 Extra Practice 1: Decoding Practice, Fluency Passage, Word Fluency A, and Activity
- Unit 5 Extra Practice 2: Decoding Practice, Fluency Passage, Word Fluency B, and Activity
- Unit 5 Extra Practice 3: Decoding Practice, Fluency Passage, Word Fluency A or B, and Activity

SCHOOL SUPPLIES

Pencils, colors (optional—markers, crayons, or colored pencils), highlighters

Important Tips

★Diagnostic–Prescriptive Teaching

SIMPLE ERRORS: WORD ENDINGS AND HIGH-FREQUENCY WORDS

With *Read Well*, most children learn to read with ease. Others need an occasional nudge or boost within the program, and a few others require diagnosis and targeted instruction.

Use the following principles to guide your instruction.

1. **STRICTLY ADHERE TO ORAL READING FLUENCY ASSESSMENT GUIDELINES**

   Passing students when they have not mastered skills, although it may seem kind, is a guarantee for later failure.

2. **USE ERROR PATTERNS TO ENHANCE INSTRUCTION**

   Use the assessments to determine what students know and what they still need to learn. Provide extra practice and reviews, as needed.

   If students fail to read with accuracy, watch for error patterns and target practice. Accuracy is needed for fluency and comprehension.

The following two boxes represent examples of error patterns and guidelines on how to correct them:

CORRECTING ERROR PATTERNS: WORD ENDINGS

Add a list of four to six words with word endings to your daily exercise. Underline the base word.

<u>Growl</u>ed, <u>growl</u>ing, <u>growl</u>s, <u>happen</u>ing, <u>happen</u>s, <u>happen</u>ed*

Tell students that careful reading of words with endings will help them read with ease and understand their stories.

For emphasis and variety, add a little rhythm to the task. Say something like:

We're going to do a little extra practice of words with endings. The endings can sneak up on us and trip us when we read.

Read each underlined word two times, then read the whole word.
My turn first. Listen: growl, growl, growled; growl, growl, growling; growl, growl, growls. Now it's your turn. Start with *growled* and keep going.

Give a few individual turns—especially to any child who has had difficulty reading words with endings.

[PJ], your turn to read the words, one time each. (growled, growling . . .)

---

* Rotate the order of the word endings so students do not get in the habit of reading in a pattern.

CORRECTING ERROR PATTERNS: HIGH-FREQUENCY WORDS

1. If students make errors on small words, remind them to read carefully during Story Reading. Their first goal is accuracy.
   - Be sure to have students finger track as they read.
   - Provide positive feedback to students who have a tendency to read carelessly. [Travis], that was perfect. You didn't let the little words catch you.
   - Have students reread sentences they read with errors. Oops, that little word *the* was tricky. Read the sentence again.

2. Keep a list of specific words missed on the Oral Reading Fluency Assessment and during any Story Reading. Put these words and the incorrect pronunciation of the words on the board (e.g., in/on, what/when, said/and, a/the). Words can also be put on cards in a pocket chart or on flash cards. Sort the words into Tricky and pattern words.

<u>wh</u>at, said, a, the, <u>in</u>, <u>on</u>, wh<u>e</u>n, <u>a</u>nd

   - For Tricky Words (what, said, a, the), underline any difficult sound. Have students identify the underlined sound, sound out the word, say the correct pronunciation of the word, spell it, and say the word again. Say something like:
     Now look at the next word. It's tricky, but you can sound it out anyway. Sound it out. (/whăăăt/) /Whăăăt/ isn't a word. How do you say it? (what) Spell *what*. (w-h-a-t) Say the word. (what)

   - For pattern words (in, on, when, and), underline any difficult sound. Have students identify the underlined sound first, then sound out the word and say it. Put both words on the board with the vowels underlined. Say something like:
     We're going to practice the little words that are easy to miss. Look at the first word. Read the underlined sound. (/ĭĭĭ/) Now sound it out and say it. (/ĭĭĭnnn/, in)

   Repeat with "on."
   Have students read the list for accuracy and fluency, as needed.

> **MULTISYLLABIC WORDS**
>
> See Unit 6 for Diagnostic–Prescriptive Tips for helping students read multisyllabic words with accuracy and ease.

How to Teach the Lessons

Teach from this section. Each instructional component is outlined in an easy-to-teach format.

Exercise 1

- Unit and Story Opener: Life as an Ant, Ant Communities
- Vocabulary
- Story Reading 1
  With the Teacher: Chapter 1
  On Your Own: Chapter 2
- Comprehension and Skill Activities 1, 2

Exercise 2a

- Exercise 2b: Focus Lesson
- Vocabulary
- Story Reading 2
  With the Teacher: Chapter 3
- Comprehension and Skill Activities 3, 4

Exercise 3

- Story Reading 3
  With the Teacher: Chapter 4
- Comprehension and Skill Activity 5a, 5b

Exercise 4

- Story Opener: An Ant With Ideas
- Vocabulary
- Story Reading 4
  With the Teacher: Chapter 1
  On Your Own: Chapter 2
- Comprehension and Skill Activities 6, 7

Exercise 5

- Story Reading 5
  With the Teacher: Chapter 3
- Comprehension and Skill Activities 8, 9a, 9b

Exercise 6

- Story Reading 6
  With the Teacher: The Lost Treasure (Fluency)
- Written Assessment

Note: Lessons include daily homework.

❶ SOUND REVIEW
Use selected Sound Cards from Units 1–4.

PACING
Exercise 1 should take about 15 minutes.

★❷ NEW SOUND INTRODUCTION
- For Row A, tell students they will learn another sound for o-w.
- Have students look at the picture. Say something like:

Look at the picture. Say "o-w says /ōōō/ as in snow." (o-w says /ōōō/ as in snow)
Listen to the o-w words in the sentence.
"We can feel the wind blow and see the snow fall."
Read the sentence. (We can feel the wind blow and see the snow fall.)
What two words have the /ōōō/ sound? (blow, snow)

- For Row B, have students read the underlined sound, then the word.
- After reading the row, have students go back and read just the words. Repeat practice.

❸ ACCURACY AND FLUENCY BUILDING
- For each task, have students say any underlined part, then read the word.
- Set a pace. Then have students read the whole words in each task and column.
- Provide repeated practice, building accuracy first, then fluency.

C1. Multisyllabic Words
- For the list of words divided by syllables, have students read and finger count each syllable, then read the word. Use the word in a sentence, as appropriate.
- For the list of whole words, build accuracy and then fluency.

E1. Tricky Words
- For each Tricky Word, have students use known sounds and word parts, then silently sound out the word. Use the word in a sentence to help with pronunciation.
- If the word is unfamiliar, tell students the word and have them say, spell, and say it.

females	Another word for *girls* is . . . *females.*
chambers	Small rooms are sometimes called . . . *chambers.*
special	I have a wonderful aunt. She is very . . . *special.*

E2. Story Words
For each word, tell students the underlined sound and have them read the word.
Use the word in a sentence, as needed.

❹ WORDS IN CONTEXT
- Tell students to use the sounds they know and the sentence to figure out each word.
Look at the first word. Sound out the word in your head.
When you think you know the word, put your thumbs up.

- Have students read the sentence. Assist, as needed.
Everyone, read the sentence. (Sam got a very special gift on her birthday.)
Read the underlined word. (special)

- Repeat with remaining words.

★ = New in this unit

★ ⑤ OPEN SYLLABLE O

- Tell students the <u>o</u> in each of these words says its name.
- Have students read the underlined sound, then the whole word.

TEAM
EXPECTATIONS
(Reminder)

Provide a quick review of expectations before starting the lesson.

1. Sit up.
2. Follow directions.
3. Help each other.
4. Work hard and have fun.

Ant Communities

Unit 5 Exercise 1
Use before Chapters 1 and 2

1. SOUND REVIEW Use selected Sound Cards from Units 1–4.

★ 2. NEW SOUND INTRODUCTION Introduce the new sound /ōōō/ as in snow.

A		
OW	sn<u>ow</u>	We can feel the wind bl<u>ow</u> and see the sn<u>ow</u> fall.

B				
gr<u>ow</u>	b<u>ow</u>l	<u>ow</u>n	foll<u>ow</u>	wind<u>ow</u>

3. ACCURACY AND FLUENCY BUILDING For each column, have students say any underlined part, then read each word. Next, have students read the whole column.

A1 Mixed Practice	B1 Word Endings	C1 Multisyllabic Words	D1 Rhyming Words	E1 Tricky Words
qu<u>ee</u>n	col·o·ny	hab·i·tat	finds	females
cl<u>ue</u>	colonies	con·struct	kinds	chambers
bod<u>y</u>		store·rooms	minds	special
gr<u>ai</u>n	nurs·er·y	thor·ax	**D2** Related Words	**E2** Story Words
l<u>ea</u>ve	nurseries	ab·do·men	survive	t<u>i</u>ny
tr<u>ai</u>l	com·mu·ni·ty	a·nat·o·my	survives	sin<u>ce</u>
gu<u>ar</u>d	communities	habitat	survivor	<u>kn</u>ow
A2 Bossy E	thou·sand	construct	survivors	
t<u>a</u>ste	thousands	storerooms		
b<u>a</u>the		thorax		
th<u>e</u>se	an·ten·na	abdomen		
	antennas	anatomy		

4. WORDS IN CONTEXT Have students use the sounds and word parts they know and then the sentences to pronounce each underlined word.

A	spe·cial	Sam got a very <u>special</u> gift on her birthday.
B	di·no·saurs	T. rex is one of my favorite <u>dinosaurs</u>.
C	mil·lions	Many people live in America. <u>Millions</u> of people live there.
D	la·bel	We need to <u>label</u> the picture.

★ 5. OPEN SYLLABLE <u>O</u> Have students practice reading /ō/ and the related words.

o	<u>o</u>·ver	<u>o</u>·pen	m<u>o</u>·ment	hip·p<u>o</u>	fr<u>o</u>·zen

BUILD ACCURACY
AND FLUENCY

For all rows and columns, follow the specific directions, then build accuracy and fluency with whole words.

ACKNOWLEDGE
STUDENTS WHEN
THEY MEET YOUR
EXPECTATIONS

Students respond positively when you acknowledge their accomplishments. Pair descriptive praise with an individual turn or job.
[Ethan], great job. You had your finger under each word that we read. Everyone, watch how [Ethan] tracks while I read the column.

COMPREHENSION PROCESSES
Remember, Understand, Apply

PROCEDURES

1. Introducing the Storybook and Theme

Identifying—Title; Defining and Using Vocabulary—community; Using Table of Contents; Describing; Inferring

• Tell students the title of their new storybook is *Communities*. Say something like:

Everyone, look at the cover of the book.
The title of this book is *Communities*.
What's the title of the book? (Communities)

⭐ A community is a group of living things that live and work together. Do people live and work together? (yes)
Yes, people live and work together. We live in communities.

What do you see on the cover? (a lot of ants, a pile of ants)
That's right. Ants live and work together. These ants are all in a big pile. I wonder what they are trying to do. What do you think?

• Have students use the Table of Contents. Say something like:
Turn to page 3.
What's on this page?
(the Table of Contents)

Our new unit is called "Life as an Ant." Touch the unit title.

The first story is called "Ant Communities." What page does it start on? (page 7)
Turn to page 7.

TABLE OF CONTENTS
UNIT 5 • Life as an Ant

3

⭐ = New in this unit

UNIT AND STORY OPENER • Life as an Ant, Ant Communities

2. Introducing the Unit and Story

Identifying—Title, Author; Classifying—Genre

Have students review the title, then identify the author.
Say something like:

Now look at page 7. What's the title? (Ant Communities)

Who is the author? (Lucy Bledsoe)

Look at the picture. It's the same picture as the cover of our book.

Do you think this passage is fact or fiction? (fact)

Passages that are made up of facts are called *nonfiction*.

What kind of passage are we going to read today? (nonfiction)

⭐ 3. Introducing K-W-L (modified)

Priming Background Knowledge; Asking Questions

- Use chart paper or three columns
  on a chalkboard to make a K-W-L Chart.

Ants		
What do we think we know?	**What do we want to know?**	**What did we learn?**
Insects (Ms. Mak)	How long have ants lived on Earth? (Ms. Mak)	
6 legs (Jon)	What do they eat? (Lee)	
Red or black (Angie)	Are they herbivores, carnivores, or omnivores? (Jorge)	
Small (Jack)		
Like sweets (Lee)		

- Demonstrate and explain that it's okay to make corrections in our knowledge. Then have students identify what they think they know about ants.

  Reading nonfiction is always fun. Sometimes we learn new facts that make us change the way we think about things. I think ants are insects. I'm going to write that on the board. What do you think you already know about ants?

- Think aloud as you demonstrate how to ask questions. Then have students generate questions about ants. Say something like:

  I wonder how long ants have lived on Earth. I've heard that they've lived on Earth for millions of years. My question is "How long have ants lived on Earth?"

COMPREHENSION PROCESSES
Understand, Apply, Evaluate

PROCEDURES

Introducing Vocabulary

> ☆ **survive, habitat** ☆ **except**
> ☆ **community** ☆ **colony**

- For each vocabulary word, have students read the word by parts, then read the whole word.
- Read the student-friendly explanations to students as they follow with their fingers. Then have students use the vocabulary word by following the gray text.
- Review and discuss the photos.

USING
VOCABULARY

WITH THE TEACHER

Chapters 1, 2

Vocabulary

★ **sur·vive**

Survive means to stay alive.

People need food and water to *survive*. What do you think animals need to survive?**1**

hab·i·tat

The place where an animal or plant lives and grows is called its **habitat**.

A hippo's *habitat* is near rivers in Africa. What is a shark's habitat?**2**

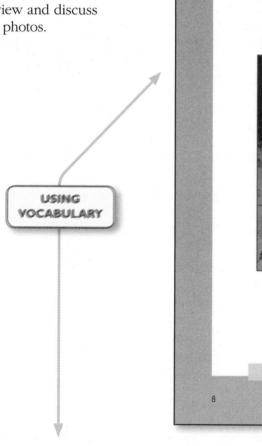

★ = New

8

1 **Apply:** Inferring, Priming Background Knowledge, Using Vocabulary—survive (They need food and water to survive.)

2 **Apply:** Inferring, Priming Background Knowledge, Using Vocabulary—habitat (A shark's habitat is the ocean.)

☆ = New in this unit

ANT COMMUNITIES

★ **ex·cept**

Except is a short way of saying "everything but" or "everywhere but."

I like all vegetables *except* broccoli. Do I like broccoli? Complete this sentence: I like to eat everything . . . **1**

★ **com·mu·ni·ty**

A **community** is a group of people or animals that lives and works together.

Our school is a *community*. Why is our school a community? **2**

★ **col·o·ny**

A **colony** is a group of animals that lives together.

Complete this sentence: Thousands of ants live together in a . . . **3**

USING VOCABULARY

9

1 **Evaluate:** Responding; **Apply:** Using Vocabulary—except (except peanuts, broccoli . . .)

2 **Apply:** Inferring, Making Connections; **Understand:** Defining Vocabulary— community (People work together at our school.)

3 **Remember:** Identifying—What; Using Vocabulary—colony (colony)

CHAPTER 1 INSTRUCTIONS

Students read Chapter 1 with the teacher and Chapter 2 on their own. *Note:* If you're working on an 8- to 11-Day Plan, you will read Chapter 2 with students.

COMPREHENSION PROCESSES

Remember, Understand, Apply

COMPREHENSION BUILDING

- Encourage students to answer questions with complete sentences.
- If students have difficulty comprehending, think aloud with them or reread the portion of the story that answers the question. Repeat the question.

PROCEDURES

1. **Introducing Chapter 1**

   Identifying—Title, Heading
   - Have students read the title and answer the gray text questions.
   - ★ Introduce headings. Say something like:

     Put your finger on the words "Ant Anatomy." This is called a *heading*.
     It tells what you will read about. What is "Ant Anatomy"? (a heading)

2. **First Reading**
   - Ask questions and discuss the story as indicated by the gray text.
   - Mix group and individual turns, independent of your voice.
     Have students work toward a group accuracy goal of 0–2 errors.
     Quietly keep track of errors made by all students in the group.
   - After reading the story, practice any difficult words.
     Reread the story if students have not reached the accuracy goal.

3. **Second Reading, Short Passage Practice: Developing Prosody**
   - Demonstrate expressive, fluent reading of the first paragraph.
     Read at a rate slightly faster than the students' rate. Say something like:

     Listen to my expression as I read the first paragraph.

     I'm going to read in a serious voice because this is nonfiction.

     I think I can make it sound like I'm reading on a TV science show.

     I'm going to read the first sentence like a question, and I'm going to pause at periods and commas.

     "Did you know that ants are insects? Like all insects, they have six legs and three main body parts. All ants have a head, a thorax, and an . . . "

   - Guide practice with your voice.
   - Provide individual turns while others track with their fingers and whisper read.
   - Repeat with one paragraph at a time. Repeat steps with each remaining paragraph.

> **REPEATED READINGS**
>
> **Prosody (Reminder)**
>
> On the second reading, students practice developing prosody— phrasing and expression. Research has shown that prosody is related to both fluency and comprehension.

★ = New in this unit

WITH THE TEACHER

Chapter 1

Ant Facts

Ant Anatomy

Did you know that ants are insects? Like all insects, they have six legs and three main body parts. All ants have a head, a thorax, and an abdomen. Ants also have antennas on their heads. Antennas help them hear, taste, and smell.

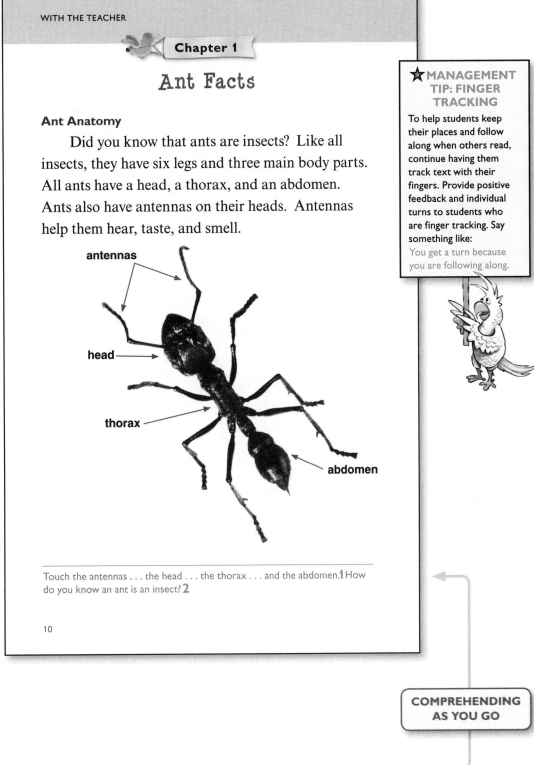

antennas

head

thorax

abdomen

Touch the antennas . . . the head . . . the thorax . . . and the abdomen.**1** How do you know an ant is an insect? **2**

10

COMPREHENDING AS YOU GO

❶ **Remember:** Identifying
❷ **Understand:** Explaining (An ant is an insect because it has six legs and three main body parts.)

ANT COMMUNITIES

Survivors

There are around 20,000 different kinds of ants. These amazing insects have been on Earth for millions of years. Ants have been on Earth since the dinosaurs. They can survive in any habitat except where it is frozen year round.

Like all living things, ants need other living things to survive. Just like people, these tiny insects live and work together in communities.

Community

One ant, two ants, three ants, four,
My, oh my, there are hundreds more.
Hundreds and thousands of ants in a nest,
Working together is always best.

K-W-L CHART
Verifying Information

After reading page 11, verify facts in the first column of the K-W-L chart. Say something like: I said that ants were insects. Did we learn from the book that ants are insects? (yes) My fact was correct. It was found in the book. It was verified.

Have students verify other information on the K-W-L chart.

What are some facts that make an ant an *amazing* animal? **1**

11

COMPREHENDING AS YOU GO

1 **Apply:** Inferring; Explaining—Facts; Using Vocabulary—amazing (Ants are amazing because they live in communities. They have lived on Earth for millions of years. Ants can survive anywhere except where the ground is frozen all the time . . .)

CHAPTER 2 INSTRUCTIONS

Students read without the teacher, independently or with partners.
Note: If you're working on an 8- to 11-Day Plan, you will read this chapter with your students.

COMPREHENSION PROCESSES

Remember, Apply

PREP NOTE

Setting a Purpose

Write questions on a chalkboard, white board, or large piece of paper before working with your group.

PROCEDURES FOR READING ON YOUR OWN

☆ 1. Getting Ready

Have students turn to "Ant Communities," Chapter 2, on page 12.

☆ 2. Setting a Purpose

Describing, Explaining

Establish a purpose for reading. Say something like:

You're going to learn why ants are very special insects. Unlike many insects, ants live and work together. Read to find out the answers to these questions:

- What is an ant colony like?
- What is an ant's nest like?
- What do worker ants do to care for the queen?
- Why are female (or girl) ants so important to the nest?

☆ FIRST ON YOUR OWN

This may be your students' first On-Your-Own reading.

- Guide practice and provide positive, descriptive feedback.
- Be sure to have students finger track so you can monitor student engagement.

3. Reading on Your Own: Partner or Whisper Reading

- Have students take turns reading every other page with a partner or have students whisper read pages 12–14 on their own.
- Continue having students track each word with their fingers.

For Whisper Reading, say something like:

Everyone, turn to page 12. This is where you're going to start reading on your own—without me. Whisper read as you track with your finger, so I can see where you are in your work. Ask and think about the gray text questions. You get to be your own teacher.

Turn to page 14. That's where you are going to stop reading.

Now turn back to page 12.

For Partner Reading, say something like:

Everyone, turn to page 12. This is where you're going to start Partner Reading. Where are you going to sit? (at our desks, side by side)

You will take turns reading pages. If you are the listener, what will you do? (keep my book flat, follow with my finger, compliment my partner)

You also get to be the teacher and ask the gray text questions.

If you are the reader, what will you do? (keep my book flat, finger track, read quietly)

☆ 4. Comprehension and Skill Work

For students on a 6-Day Plan, tell them they will do Comprehension and Skill Activities 1 and 2 after they read on their own. Guide practice, as needed. For teacher directions, see pages 27 and 28. (For 8- to 11-Day Plans, see the Lesson Planner, page 7.)

5. Homework 1: Repeated Reading

☆ = New in this unit

COMPREHENDING
AS YOU GO

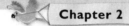 **Chapter 2**

Colonies

What do you know about ant anatomy?**1** What facts make these insects amazing animals?**2**

Ants live and work together in communities called colonies. Thousands of ants may live in one colony.

The Nest

If you see a trail of ants, they may be on their way to their front door. The ant colony lives in a nest. The nest is like an underground apartment building with many rooms. These rooms are called chambers.

Look at the picture. Where do ants live?**3** Where do you think the trail of ants will lead?**4**

12

1 Understand: Summarizing—Facts (Ants have six legs and three body parts. Ants have a head, a thorax, and an abdomen. Ants have antennas on their heads.)

2 Apply: Inferring; **Understand:** Summarizing—Facts; Using Vocabulary—amazing (Ants are amazing because they live in colonies . . .)

3 Remember: Identifying—Where; Using Vocabulary—community, colony (Ants live in communities called colonies. The colony lives in a nest.)

4 Apply: Inferring (The trail of ants will lead back to the nest.)

ANT COMMUNITIES

The nest has special chambers for different things—storerooms for food, nurseries for baby ants, rooms for resting, and rooms for trash. The queen ant has her own chamber.

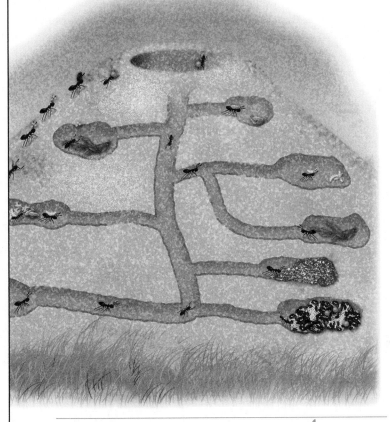

Why do you think the queen has her own special chamber? **1**

13

COMPREHENDING AS YOU GO

1 **Apply:** Inferring (She is the most important ant. She is the queen . . .)

ON YOUR OWN

The Queen of the Colony

Most colonies have one queen. The queen ant is the biggest ant in the colony. Worker ants build a nest for her. The workers feed, guard, and even bathe her.

The queen's job is to lay tiny eggs. Each egg is as small as a grain of sand. Most of the eggs will hatch into female ants. Females are the workers, so many female ants are needed for the colony to survive.

What is the queen's job?¹ How do the workers take care of the queen?² Why are most ants females?³

14

COMPREHENDING
AS YOU GO

❶ **Remember:** Identifying—What (The queen's job is to lay eggs.)
❷ **Remember:** Identifying—How (They build a nest for her. They feed, guard, and bathe her.)
❸ **Apply:** Inferring; Explaining; Using Vocabulary—survive (Females are the workers. Many workers are needed for the colony to survive.)

Identifying—Fact

Identifying—What

Identifying—Topic

Drawing Conclusions

Inferring—Main Idea

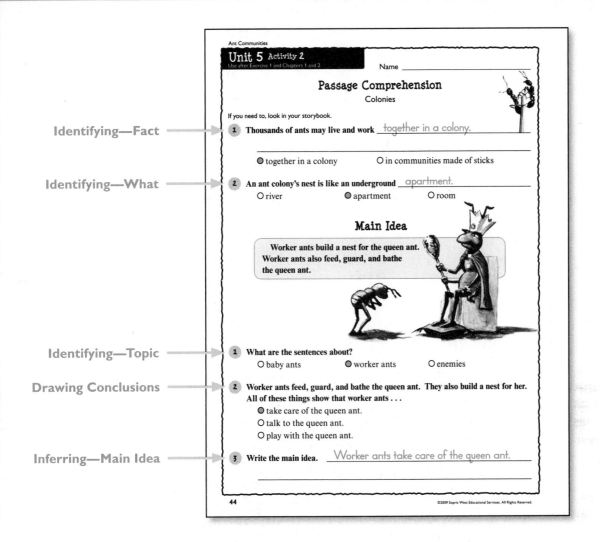

Ant Communities

Unit 5 Activity 2
Use after Exercise 1 and Chapters 1 and 2

Name _____

Passage Comprehension
Colonies

If you need to, look in your storybook.

1 Thousands of ants may live and work _together in a colony._
_____

● together in a colony   ○ in communities made of sticks

2 An ant colony's nest is like an underground _apartment._
○ river   ● apartment   ○ room

Main Idea

Worker ants build a nest for the queen ant.
Worker ants also feed, guard, and bathe
the queen ant.

1 What are the sentences about?
○ baby ants   ● worker ants   ○ enemies

2 Worker ants feed, guard, and bathe the queen ant. They also build a nest for her.
All of these things show that worker ants . . .
● take care of the queen ant.
○ talk to the queen ant.
○ play with the queen ant.

3 Write the main idea. _Worker ants take care of the queen ant._
_____

44

❶ SOUND REVIEW

Use selected Sound Cards from Units 1–5.

PACING

Exercises 2a and 2b should take about 20 minutes.

❷ SHIFTY WORD BLENDING

For each word, have students say the underlined sound. Then have them sound out the word smoothly and say it. Use the words in sentences, as needed.

❸ ACCURACY AND FLUENCY BUILDING

- For each task, have students say any underlined part, then read the word.
- Set a pace. Then have students read the whole words in each task and column.
- Provide repeated practice, building accuracy first, then fluency.

B1. Reading by Analogy

Have students figure out how to say o-l and -al by reading other words they know.

C1. Multisyllabic Words

- For the list of words divided by syllables, have students read the underlined part, read each syllable out loud, then finger count the syllables. Use the word in a sentence, as appropriate. Have students identify what's the same about the first three words.

adventure	3 syllables	Miss Tam went on an . . . *adventure.*
picture	2 syllables	I got the camera so I could take a . . . *picture.*
temperature	4 syllables	It wasn't hot or cold. The . . . *temperature* . . . was just right.
larvas	2 syllables	When insects hatch, they look like little worms called . . . *larvas.*
nursery	3 syllables	Babies are taken care of in a . . . *nursery.*

- For the list of whole words, build accuracy and then fluency.

D1. Word Endings

Have students read each set of words. Tell students you change the y to i and add e-s when you change "body" to "bodies" and "butterfly" to "butterflies."

E1. Tricky Words

- For each Tricky Word, have students use known sounds and word parts, then silently sound out the word. Use the word in a sentence to help with pronunciation.
- If the word is unfamiliar, tell students the word and have them say, spell, and say it.

pupas	After the larval stage, insects become . . . *pupas.*
chambers	The heart has four . . . *chambers.*
cycle	All animals have a life . . . *cycle.*

E2. Story Words

For each word, tell students the underlined sound and have them read the word.

stage	In an ant's life cycle, an egg is the first . . . *stage.*
change	Steve got his clothes wet, so he had to . . . *change.*
ready	It's time to go. Are you . . . *ready?*
metamorphosis	The change an insect goes through is called . . . *metamorphosis.*

❹ WORDS IN CONTEXT

⑤ **OPEN SYLLABLE O**
- Tell students the <u>o</u> in each of these words says its name.
- Have students read any underlined part, then the word.

Ant Communities

Unit 5 Exercise 2a
Use before Exercise 2b (Focus Lesson)

1. SOUND REVIEW Have students review sounds for accuracy, then for fluency.

Ⓐ	ow as in snow	ue as in blue	u as in umbrella	o as in otter	
Ⓑ	aw	ou	ir	ew	wh	er

2. SHIFTY WORD BLENDING For each word, have students say the underlined part, sound out smoothly, then read the word.

s<u>pin</u>	s<u>kin</u>	<u>sh</u>in	<u>th</u>in	<u>th</u>i<u>s</u>

3. ACCURACY AND FLUENCY BUILDING For each column, have students say any underlined part, then read each word. Next, have students read the whole column.

A1 New Sound Practice	**B1** Reading by Analogy	**C1** Multisyllabic Words	**D1** Word Endings	**E1** Tricky Words
sn<u>ow</u>	<u>old</u>	ad·ven·<u>ture</u>	body	pupas
l<u>ow</u>	f<u>old</u>	pic·<u>ture</u>	bodies	chambers
sh<u>ow</u>	m<u>ol</u>t	tem·per·a·<u>ture</u>		cycle
sl<u>ow</u>ly		lar·vas	butterfly	**E2** Story Words
gr<u>ow</u>	anim<u>al</u>	nurs·er·y	butterflies	
A2 Mixed Practice	sand<u>al</u>		baby	sta<u>ge</u>
	sever<u>al</u>	adven<u>ture</u>	babies	chan<u>ge</u>
life		pic<u>ture</u>		r<u>ea</u>dy
<u>a</u>dult		temper<u>ature</u>	colony	metamor<u>ph</u>osis
cr<u>aw</u>l		larvas	colonies	
n<u>ur</u>se		nursery		
<u>th</u>i<u>rd</u>				

4. WORDS IN CONTEXT Have students use the sounds and word parts they know and then the sentences to pronounce each underlined word.

Ⓐ	fourth	First, second, third, <u>fourth</u>.
Ⓑ	warm	The food is not too hot. It is <u>warm</u>.
Ⓒ	worms	Animals with long skinny bodies and no legs are <u>worms</u>.
Ⓓ	stomachs	Cows have <u>stomachs</u> with four chambers.
Ⓔ	cocoon	A caterpillar spins a silk <u>cocoon</u> around its body.

5. OPEN SYLLABLE O Have students practice reading /ō/ and the related words.

o	g<u>o</u>	<u>o</u>·pen	<u>o</u>·ver	pr<u>o</u>·tect

29

FACT SUMMARY

PURPOSE

This lesson provides explicit instruction in how to develop a written summary that explains why ants are insects. The lesson prepares students for Comprehension and Skill Work. Students do not write in their books, but will watch and respond as you guide them through the lesson.

COMPREHENSION PROCESSES

Remember, Understand

PROCEDURES

1. Introducing Fact Summary

Priming Background Knowledge

Introduce the Fact Summary Focus Lesson. Say something like:

Today, we're going to work on writing another fact summary.

A fact summary is a strategy for remembering and understanding what you've read.

What is a fact? (A fact is something that is real. A fact is true.)

That's right, and a fact summary is a shortened version of facts you've read about.

> **PREP NOTE**
>
> To demonstrate how to complete the matching exercise, use an overhead of the page in students' *Exercise Book 1*, write on a transparency placed over the page, or use a paper copy.

2. Identifying and Locating Facts

Identifying—Title, Facts; Locating Information

- Have students choral read the title and passage.
- Have students read Fact 1 and locate the information in the passage.

  Now, you are going to help me write a fact summary.

  Fact 1 is already written for us. Let's read that fact together.

  (Ants have three body parts.)

  Find the sentence in the passage that tells us this fact.

  Everyone, read that fact. (Like all insects, ants have three body parts.)

- Have students complete Facts 2 and 3 by locating information in the passage.

  We need to finish Fact 2. What does it say? (Ants have a head . . .)

  Find the sentence in the passage that will help us complete the fact.

  Everyone, read that fact. (They have a head, a thorax, and an abdomen.)

  What word should I write to complete the fact? (abdomen)

  What should I do if I can't remember how to spell *abdomen*?

  (Look in the passage.) **Write "abdomen" to complete Fact 2.**

  Repeat with Fact 3. **Write "six legs and two antennas" to complete Fact 3.**

- Have students read the three facts.

> **BUILDING KNOWLEDGE**
>
> **Inductive Thinking**
>
> Students' mastery of facts helps to build content knowledge.
>
> By completing fact summaries, your children will use inductive thinking to demonstrate what they've learned.

3. Summarizing

Summarizing, Explaining

Tell students the facts will help them explain what makes an ant an insect.

Put your finger on the part that says "Explain." Let's read that part together.

(Using the facts you've listed, tell why ants are insects. All ants are insects . . .)

Now we can use the facts you helped me write to explain why all ants are insects.

This will be our fact summary. Raise your hand if you can complete the sentence.

(All ants are insects because . . . they have three body parts, six legs, and two antennas.)

Ant Communities

Unit 5 Exercise **2b** (Focus Lesson)
Use after Exercise 2a and before Chapter 3

FOCUS
LESSON
Skills and
Strategies

Fact Summary

What Is An Ant?

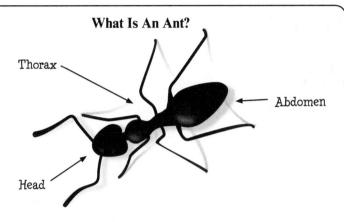

Thorax

Abdomen

Head

Like all insects, ants have three body parts. They have a head, a thorax, and an abdomen. They also have six legs and two antennas.

Fact 1:
Ants have three body parts.

Fact 2:
Ants have a head, a thorax, and an ___abdomen.___

Fact 3:
They also have ___six legs and two antennas.___

STOP
Don't write
in your
Exercise
Book.

Explain:
Using the facts you've listed, tell why ants are insects.

All ants are insects. We know they are insects because ___they have three___

___body parts, six legs, and two antennas.___

COMPREHENSION PROCESSES

Understand, Apply

PROCEDURES

Introducing Vocabulary

> ☆ life cycle
> ☆ metamorphosis ☆ molt
> ☆ protect

- For each vocabulary word, have students read the word by parts, then read the whole word.
- Read the student-friendly explanations to students as they follow with their fingers.
- Have students use the vocabulary word by following the gray text and reviewing the photos and illustrations, as appropriate.

☆ = New in this unit

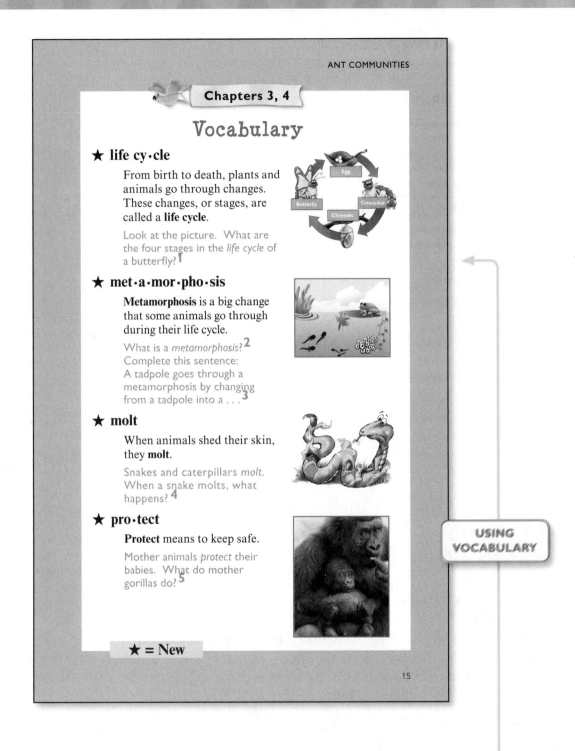

ANT COMMUNITIES

Chapters 3, 4

Vocabulary

★ **life cy·cle**

From birth to death, plants and animals go through changes. These changes, or stages, are called a **life cycle**.

Look at the picture. What are the four stages in the *life cycle* of a butterfly? **1**

★ **met·a·mor·pho·sis**

Metamorphosis is a big change that some animals go through during their life cycle.

What is a *metamorphosis*? **2** Complete this sentence: A tadpole goes through a metamorphosis by changing from a tadpole into a . . . **3**

★ **molt**

When animals shed their skin, they **molt**.

Snakes and caterpillars *molt*. When a snake molts, what happens? **4**

★ **pro·tect**

Protect means to keep safe.

Mother animals *protect* their babies. What do mother gorillas do? **5**

★ = New

15

USING VOCABULARY

❶ **Apply:** Using Graphic Organizer, Using Vocabulary—life cycle (The first stage is the egg. The next stages are the caterpillar, chrysallis, and butterfly.)

❷ **Understand:** Defining and Using Vocabulary—metamorphosis (A metamorphosis is a change that some animals go through.)

❸ **Apply:** Using Vocabulary—metamorphosis (frog)

❹ **Apply:** Using Vocabulary—molt (It sheds its skin.)

❺ **Understand:** Defining and Using Vocabulary—protect (They keep their babies safe. They protect their babies.)

CHAPTER 3 INSTRUCTIONS
Students read with the teacher.

COMPREHENSION PROCESSES
Remember, Understand, Apply

PROCEDURES

1. Reviewing Chapter 2

   Identifying—Facts; Describing; Locating Information
   Discuss questions from the board.
   You read Chapter 2 on your own. Let's talk about what you learned.
   If we can't remember, what can we do? (look in our books)
   • What is an ant colony like? (Thousands of ants live and work in a colony . . .)
   • What is an ant's nest like? (The nest has many rooms like an apartment building . . .)
   • What do worker ants do to care for the queen? (They feed, guard, and bathe her.)
   • Why are female (or girl) ants so important to the nest? (Females are the workers.)

2. Introducing Chapter 3

   Identifying—Title, Heading; Inferring
   • Have students identify the title, then ask the gray text questions to introduce the chapter.
   • Have students read the first heading. Say something like:
   Read the heading. (The Four Stages)
   What will you learn about in this section? (the four stages of an ant's life cycle)

3. First Reading
   • Ask questions and discuss the story as indicated by the gray text.
   • Mix group and individual turns, independent of your voice.
     Have students work toward a group accuracy goal of 0–2 errors.
   • After reading the story, practice any difficult words. Reread the story if students have not
     reached the accuracy goal.

4. Second Reading, Timed Readings: Repeated Reading
    • As time allows, have students do Timed Readings while others follow along.
   • Time individuals for 30 seconds and encourage each child to work for a
     personal best.
   • Count the number of words read correctly in 30 seconds (words read minus errors).
     Multiply by two to determine words correct per minute. Record student scores.

5. Partner or Whisper Reading: Repeated Reading
    Before beginning independent work, have students finger track and do Partner or
   Whisper Reading.

6. Comprehension and Skill Work
   Tell students they will do Comprehension and Skill Activities 3 and 4 after reading
   Chapter 3. Guide practice, as needed. For teacher directions, see pages 40 and 41.

7. Homework 2: Repeated Reading

WITH THE TEACHER

Chapter 3

Life Cycle

What do you know about ant colonies and the queen ant?[1] What will you learn about in this chapter? [2]

The Four Stages

Each ant has four stages in its life:

Life Cycle of Ants

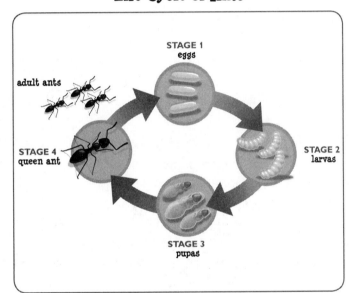

▲ Like butterflies and frogs, ants go through a big change called a *metamorphosis*.

Using the diagram above, describe the *life cycle* of ants. [3]

16

FOCUS ON VIEWING

Graphic Organizers, Identifying—Facts

After completing the page, have students touch each stage of the ant's life. Say something like:

The picture is called a cycle graph. It shows that every ant goes through four stages. Each generation of ants goes through the same stages, or cycle.

Touch the beginning of the ant's life.

What is the first stage? (eggs)

What's the next stage? (larvas)

What's the third stage? (pupas)

What's the fourth stage? (adults)

COMPREHENDING AS YOU GO

❶ Apply: Priming Background Knowledge (Ant colonies have chambers for different things. The queen ant has her own chamber. Worker ants take care of the queen. Her job is to lay eggs . . .)

❷ Apply: Inferring (We will learn about the life cycle of an ant. We'll learn what stages they go through. Maybe we'll learn about how they hatch, the babies . . .)

❸ Understand: Describing; Using Vocabulary—life cycle (The queen ant lays eggs that turn into larvas, then into pupas. Then the pupas become adult worker ants.)

ANT COMMUNITIES

STAGE 1
eggs

As soon as the queen lays her eggs, worker ants carry the eggs to the nursery. The eggs must be kept at the right temperature, so the nursery workers move the eggs to different chambers several times a day.

STAGE 2
larvas

When the eggs hatch, the baby ants look like tiny worms called larvas. The worker ants clean the larvas and keep them warm by moving them to different chambers. The workers even feed the babies food from their own stomachs.

As the larvas grow, their skin gets tight. They shed their skin and grow new skin. This is called molting. The larvas molt four or five times during this stage.

What happens to the eggs after the queen ant lays them?**1** How do the workers take care of the larvas?**2** Why do the larvas molt?**3**

17

COMPREHENDING
AS YOU GO

1 **Remember:** Identifying—Fact (The worker ants carry the eggs to the nursery.)

2 **Remember:** Identifying—How (The workers clean the larvas and keep them warm.)

3 **Apply:** Inferring; Using Vocabulary—molt (The larvas molt because their skin gets tight.)

WITH THE TEACHER

STAGE 3
pupas

During the third stage, the larvas spin cocoons around their bodies. Now the baby ants are called pupas. The pupas grow inside their cocoons. The workers also move the pupas to different chambers several times a day.

STAGE 4
adults

When the pupas have changed into adults, worker ants bite open the cocoons. During this fourth stage, the new adult ants crawl out. Soon they will be strong and ready to do their jobs within the colony.

K-W-L CHART
Verifying, Identifying, Asking Questions

After reading, have students review their K-W-L Chart.
• Put stars by facts that were verified.
• List new facts learned.
• Add new questions that students may wish to research.

What happens in stage 3?¹ Why do you think the worker ants move the pupas to different chambers?² What happens in stage 4?³

18

COMPREHENDING AS YOU GO

❶ **Remember:** Identifying—Fact (The larvas spin cocoons around their bodies.)

❷ **Apply:** Inferring (The workers move the pupas to keep them warm.)

❸ **Remember:** Identifying—Fact (In stage 4, the workers bite open the cocoons when the pupas have changed into adults.)

PASSAGE COMPREHENSION

COMPREHENSION PROCESSES

Remember, Understand, Apply

WRITING TRAITS

Conventions—Complete Sentence, Beginning Capital, Period

Identifying—What
Using Vocabulary—metamorphosis

Using Graphic Organizer; Illustrating
Using Vocabulary—life cycle

Identifying—Facts

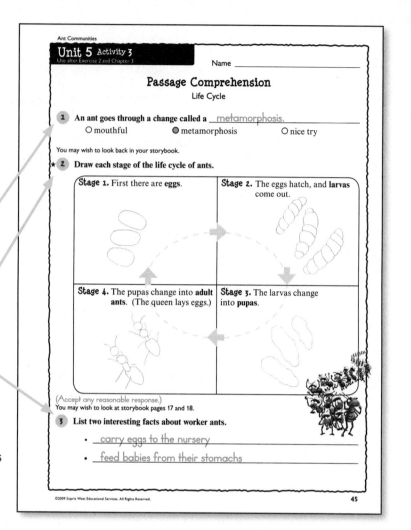

Ant Communities

Unit 5 Activity **3**
Use after Exercise 2 and Chapter 3

Name _____

Passage Comprehension
Life Cycle

1 An ant goes through a change called a __metamorphosis.__
○ mouthful ● metamorphosis ○ nice try

You may wish to look back in your storybook.

★ **2** Draw each stage of the life cycle of ants.

Stage 1. First there are eggs.

Stage 2. The eggs hatch, and **larvas** come out.

Stage 4. The pupas change into **adult ants.** (The queen lays eggs.)

Stage 3. The larvas change into **pupas.**

(Accept any reasonable response.)
You may wish to look at storybook pages 17 and 18.

3 List two interesting facts about worker ants.

• __carry eggs to the nursery__

• __feed babies from their stomachs__

45

PROCEDURES

For each step, demonstrate and guide practice, as needed. Then have students complete the page independently.

1. Selection Response—Basic Instructions (Item 1)
Have students read the sentence starter, then fill in the bubble and blank with the correct answer. Remind students to put a period at the end of sentences.

2. Cycle Graph—Specific Instructions (Item 2)
Have students read the sentence and illustrate each stage in the life cycle of an ant.
For each stage, say something like:
Follow the arrows and the dotted lines with your finger.
What do the arrows do? (go in a circle)
You are going to draw each stage of the life cycle of an ant.
The cycle goes in a circle from egg to adult. Read the sentence for stage 1.
(First there are eggs.)
What should you draw to illustrate the first stage? (eggs)
Read the next sentence. (The eggs hatch, and larvas come out.)

3. Making Lists—Basic Instructions (Item 3)
• Have students read directions and brainstorm possible answers.
• Have students write the answers in the blanks.

Self-monitoring
Have students check and correct their work.

PASSAGE READING FLUENCY

FLUENCY

Accuracy, Expression, Rate

PROCEDURES

For each step, demonstrate and guide practice, as needed. Then have students complete the page independently.

Passage Reading—Basic Instructions

- Have students read the practice words.
- Have students finger track and whisper read the story two times—the first time for accuracy and the second for expression. Have students cross out an ant each time they finish.
- Have students do a one-minute Timed Reading. Have students cross out the timer when they finish. Say something like:

You are going to track with your finger and whisper read.

You are going to read the passage three times.

The first time, read for accuracy. What will you read for? (accuracy)

The second time, read for accuracy and expression. What will you read for? (accuracy and expression)

Each time you read, cross out an ant and notice how much better your reading sounds.

The last time you read, use the timer. Read quickly, but accurately and with expression.

See if you can finish reading before one minute is up.

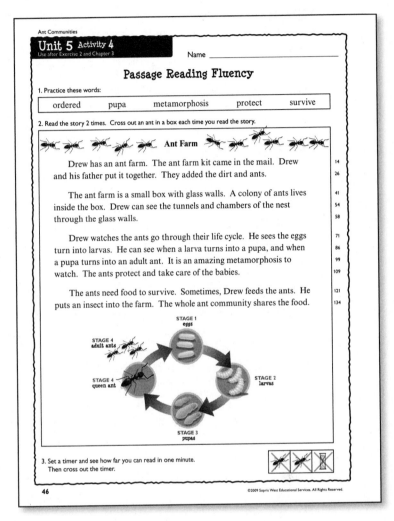

Ant Communities

Unit 5 Activity 4
Use after Exercise 2 and Chapter 3

Name _____

Passage Reading Fluency

1. Practice these words:

| ordered | pupa | metamorphosis | protect | survive |

2. Read the story 2 times. Cross out an ant in a box each time you read the story.

Ant Farm

Drew has an ant farm. The ant farm kit came in the mail. Drew and his father put it together. They added the dirt and ants. — 14 / 26

The ant farm is a small box with glass walls. A colony of ants lives inside the box. Drew can see the tunnels and chambers of the nest through the glass walls. — 41 / 54 / 58

Drew watches the ants go through their life cycle. He sees the eggs turn into larvas. He can see when a larva turns into a pupa, and when a pupa turns into an adult ant. It is an amazing metamorphosis to watch. The ants protect and take care of the babies. — 71 / 86 / 99 / 109

The ants need food to survive. Sometimes, Drew feeds the ants. He puts an insect into the farm. The whole ant community shares the food. — 121 / 134

STAGE 1 eggs
STAGE 4 adult ants
STAGE 4 queen ant
STAGE 2 larvas
STAGE 3 pupas

3. Set a timer and see how far you can read in one minute. Then cross out the timer.

46

©2009 Sopris West Educational Services. All Rights Reserved.

❶ SOUND REVIEW
Use selected Sound Cards from Units 1–5.

❷ SOUND PRACTICE
- For each task, have students spell and say the focus sound in the gray bar.
- Next, have students read each underlined sound, the word, then the whole column.

❸ ACCURACY AND FLUENCY BUILDING
- For each task, have students say any underlined part, then read the word.
- Set a pace. Then have students read the whole words in each task and column.

C1. Multisyllabic Words
- For the list of words divided by syllables, have students read each syllable, then read the word. Use the word in a sentence, as appropriate.

caterpillar	Before the insect became a butterfly, it was a . . . *caterpillar.*
liquids	Water and orange juice are . . . *liquids.*
colony	The group of ants lived in a . . . *colony.*

- For the list of whole words, build accuracy and then fluency.

E1. Tricky Words
- For each Tricky Word, have students use known sounds and word parts, then silently sound out the word. Use the word in a sentence to help with pronunciation.
- If the word is unfamiliar, tell students the word and have them say, spell, and say it.

weight	Body builders can lift a lot of . . . *weight.*
above	I could see a plane in the sky . . . *above.*
duty	The nurse took care of the patients. That was her . . . *duty.*
swarm	The bees got upset and started to . . . *swarm.*
danger	If there is a hurricane, there is . . . *danger.*

E2. Story Words
For each word, tell students the underlined sound and have them read the word.

d<u>ea</u>d	When something is no longer living, it is . . . *dead.*
change	I spilled milk all over me, so I need to . . . *change.*
<u>kn</u>ow	We can read big words. We . . . *know* . . . how to read.

❹ MORPHOGRAPHS AND AFFIXES

❺ WORDS IN CONTEXT

❻ MORPHOGRAPHS
☆Introduce the morphograph *-ful.* Say something like:
Everyone, read Row A. (-ful equals full of. Colorful equals full of color . . .)
- Have students rephrase the sentence.
  Listen to the sentence again. "The painting was so colorful."
  That means the painting was . . . full of color.
- Repeat with "careful equals full of care."

☆ = New in this unit

Ant Communities

Unit 5 Exercise 3
Use before Chapter 4

1. SOUND REVIEW Use selected Sound Cards from Units 1–5.

2. SOUND PRACTICE In each column, have students spell and say the sound, then say any underlined sound and the word. Next, have students read the whole column.

ow as in snow	Bossy <u>E</u>	**a** as in ago	**aw**
<u>ow</u>n	b<u>i</u>te	<u>a</u>ttack	cl<u>aw</u>
foll<u>ow</u>	w<u>a</u>ve	<u>a</u>maze	dr<u>aw</u>
gr<u>ow</u>	c<u>a</u>re	extr<u>a</u>	str<u>aw</u>

3. ACCURACY AND FLUENCY BUILDING For each column, have students say any underlined part, then read each word. Next, have students read the whole column.

A1 Mixed Practice	**B1** Related Words	**C1** Multisyllabic Words	**D1** Word Endings	**E1** Tricky Words
smelly	work	cat•er•pil•lar	drag	weight
alw<u>ay</u>s	worker	li•quids	dragging	above
f<u>ou</u>nd	working	col•o•ny		duty
gu<u>ar</u>d	**B2** Compound Words		make	swarm
<u>ch</u>unks	anthill	caterpillar	making	danger
p<u>a</u><u>th</u>	cleanup	liquids		**E2** Story Words
pr<u>o</u>tect	outside	colony	enemy	dead
		C2 Rhyming Words	enemies	chan<u>ge</u>
		kinds	community	<u>kn</u>ow
		minds	communities	
		finds		

4. MORPHOGRAPHS AND AFFIXES Have students read the underlined word part, then the word.

<u>re</u>turns	<u>un</u>used	construc<u>tion</u>	amazing<u>ly</u>

5. WORDS IN CONTEXT Have students use the sounds and word parts they know and then the sentences to pronounce each underlined word.

A	en•trance	I went into the room through the <u>entrance</u>.
B	warn	The fire alarm will <u>warn</u> us of danger.
C	ser•vice	We got our food right away. The waiter gave us good <u>service</u>.

6. MORPHOGRAPHS Have students practice reading "-ful = full of" and the related words and sentences.

A ★ -ful = full of	colorful = full of color	The painting was so <u>colorful</u>.
B	careful = full of care	Be <u>careful</u> when you cross the street.

31

CHAPTER 4 INSTRUCTIONS
Students read Chapter 4 with the teacher.

COMPREHENSION PROCESSES
Remember, Understand, Apply

PROCEDURES

★ **1. Previewing Chapter 4**

Identifying—Title, Headings; Using Vocabulary—communities;
Inferring; Previewing

• Preview Chapter 4 by reading the title and chapter headings. Say something like:

Turn to page 19. What's the title of the chapter? (Working Together)
Ants live and work together. They work in . . . (communities).

Good readers often use a strategy called previewing. *Previewing* means to look ahead. Good readers preview so they can tell what we are going to read about. What are we going to do? (preview, look ahead, find out what we are going to read about)

Read the first heading. (A Community of Workers)
Headings often give you a hint about a section. What do you think we'll learn about in this section? (what the workers do, how they work together . . .)

Read the next heading. (Construction)
Construction workers build things. Some ants must be . . . construction workers.

• Repeat with each heading on pages 20–22.

2. First Reading
• Ask questions and discuss the text as indicated by the gray text.
• Mix group and individual turns, independent of your voice.
• After reading the story, practice any difficult words and reread, if appropriate.

3. Second Reading, Short Passage Practice: Developing Prosody
• Demonstrate expressive, fluent reading of the first two paragraphs.
• Guide practice with your voice.
• Provide individual turns while others track with their fingers and whisper read.
• Repeat with one paragraph or page at a time.

4. Partner or Whisper Reading: Repeated Reading
 Before beginning independent work, have students finger track and do Partner or Whisper Reading.

5. Comprehension and Skill Work
Tell students they will do Comprehension and Skill Activity 5a and 5b after they read Chapter 4. Guide practice, as needed. For teacher directions, see pages 49 and 50.

6. Homework 3: Repeated Reading

★ = New in this unit

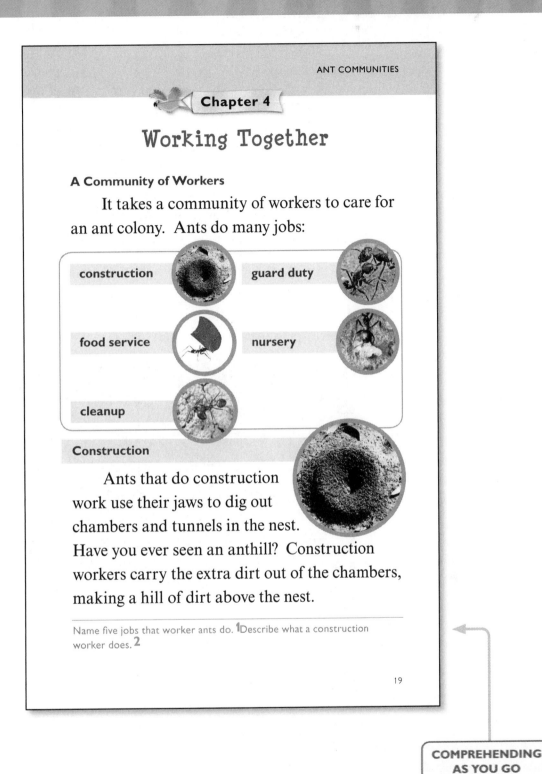

ANT COMMUNITIES

Chapter 4

Working Together

A Community of Workers

It takes a community of workers to care for an ant colony. Ants do many jobs:

construction		guard duty
food service		nursery
cleanup		

Construction

Ants that do construction work use their jaws to dig out chambers and tunnels in the nest. Have you ever seen an anthill? Construction workers carry the extra dirt out of the chambers, making a hill of dirt above the nest.

Name five jobs that worker ants do. **1** Describe what a construction worker does. **2**

19

COMPREHENDING
AS YOU GO

❶ **Remember:** Identifying—Facts (construction, food service, cleanup, guard duty, nursery)
❷ **Understand:** Describing (Construction workers use their jaws to dig chambers and tunnels in the nest.)

WITH THE TEACHER

Food Service

Many workers are needed to gather food. Finding food is dangerous because the ants must leave the safety of their nest. Some ants hunt. Some collect seeds and sweet liquids from plants. Ants look for food wherever it can be found.

Ants wave their antennas in the air looking for food. When an ant finds food, it returns to the nest, dragging its body on the ground. This makes a smelly path that other ants can follow.

MOTIVATE STUDENTS' INTEREST

After completing the page, say something like:
There were facts in this section that I didn't know. I didn't know how ants let other ants know where food was. It's pretty amazing.

Describe what worker ants do to find food. **1**

20

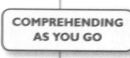

COMPREHENDING AS YOU GO

❶ **Understand:** Describing (Ants leave the nest and wave their antennas in the air to find food. When they find food, they make a path back to the nest so other ants can follow them to the food.)

ANT COMMUNITIES

Ants drag big chunks of food back to their nest. Little ants are amazingly strong. They can lift 10 times their own weight!

Cleanup

Some workers clean the nest, taking unused food and even dead ants to the nest's dump. The dump may be inside or outside the nest.

Describe what is happening in the picture.**1** Could you walk home with a bag full of groceries that weighed as much as 10 of your friends?**2**

21

MODEL ENTHUSIASM!
Making Connections
To encourage students' interest in nonfiction, model enthusiasm. Say something like:
I am fascinated by ants! It's hard to believe these little creatures can have jobs just like people.

If you were an ant, what job would you want?

COMPREHENDING AS YOU GO

❶ **Understand:** Viewing, Describing (Ants are carrying food back to their nest.)
❷ **Apply:** Making Connections (No way!)

WITH THE TEACHER

Guard Duty

Some worker ants protect the nest. They stand near the entrance to watch out for other animals and ants that don't belong.

If danger is near, these ants let out a strong smell to warn the other ants. Ants on guard duty may even attack enemies.

Nursery

Nursery workers take care of the eggs, larvas, and pupas by keeping them warm and well fed.

Busy Communities

Tiny ant communities are busy, busy places. Every ant has a job.

If you were an ant, what job would you want?

K-W-L
(modified)

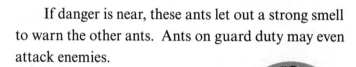

Ants		
What do we think we <u>k</u>now?	What do we <u>w</u>ant to know?	What did we <u>l</u>earn?

22

K-W-L CHART
Identifying—Facts; Verifying; Asking Questions

After reading, have students review their K-W-L Chart. While reviewing the headings and what was learned:
• put stars by facts that were verified.
• list new facts learned.
• add new questions that students may wish to research.

FACT SUMMARY

COMPREHENSION PROCESSES

Remember, Understand, Apply, Evaluate, Create

WRITING TRAITS

Conventions—Complete Sentence, Beginning Capital, Period

Identifying—Facts

Explaining

Using Graphic Organizer; Illustrating Identifying—What

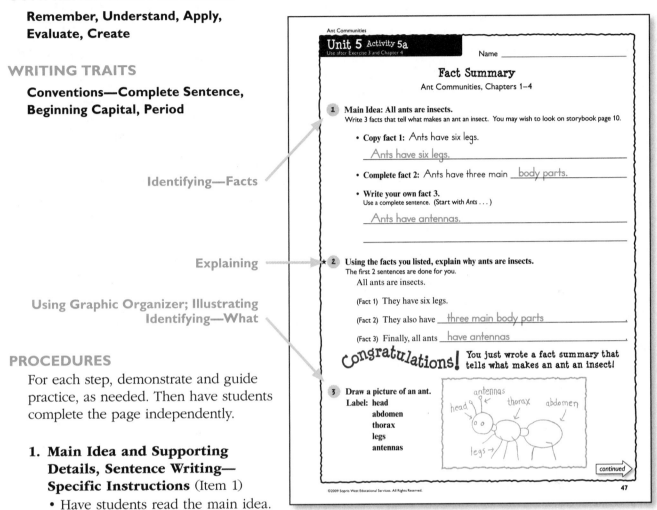

PROCEDURES

For each step, demonstrate and guide practice, as needed. Then have students complete the page independently.

1. **Main Idea and Supporting Details, Sentence Writing— Specific Instructions** (Item 1)
   - Have students read the main idea.
   - Tell students they are going to write three facts that explain what makes an ant an insect. Have students read Fact 1 and tell them they will copy that fact on the line.
   - Have students read the beginning of Fact 2 and orally complete the sentence. Have students write their answers in the blank. Remind them that they can look in their storybook on page 10 for help.
   - For Fact 3, have students orally identify another fact that explains what makes an ant an insect. Remind students to use the sentence starter in the parentheses to write a good sentence.

2. **Fact Summary, Sentence Completion—Specific Instructions** (Item 2)
   - Tell students they will complete their fact summary in Item 2 by using the facts they know to explain what makes an ant an insect.
   - Have students read and fill in the writing frame.

3. **Diagram, Illustrating, Labeling—Specific Instructions** (Item 3)
   - Have students read Item 3.
   - Tell students they will draw an ant and label the body parts listed. Demonstrate, as needed.

FACT SUMMARY (*continued*)

⭐ **4. Chart—Introductory Instructions** (Item 4)
  • Introduce the matrix. Say something like:
    This chart organizes information in rows and in columns.
    Touch the word *Job* at the top of the first column. Each box in that
    column is about a job that an ant might have. What are the jobs?
    (construction worker, cleanup worker . . .)

    Touch the header in Column 2. Now read it. (What is the worker's
    responsibility?)
    Each box below in the second column will describe the
    responsibilities of a worker ant.
    Find the construction worker. Now look in the box in the next
    column to find out what it does.
    What does a construction worker do? (dig out chambers and
    tunnels)
    Excellent! You used the chart to find out what a construction worker does.

    You can read the columns to tell what? (the jobs and responsibilities an ant might have)
    You can read the rows to tell what job . . . each ant has.

  • Have students fill in the boxes in Column 2.

CHECKOUT OPPORTUNITY

Listen to your students read individually while others work. When possible, provide your lowest-performing students with one-to-one practice.

5. Sentence Completion—Basic Instructions (Items 5, 6)
  Have students read and complete each sentence stem. Remind students to write a complete
  sentence and to put a period at the end of sentences.

⭐ = New in this unit

FACT SUMMARY (continued)

Using Graphic
Organizer
Identifying—Facts
Using Vocabulary—
responsible,
responsibility

Responding

Responding
Explaining
Generating Ideas—
Open-Ended Response

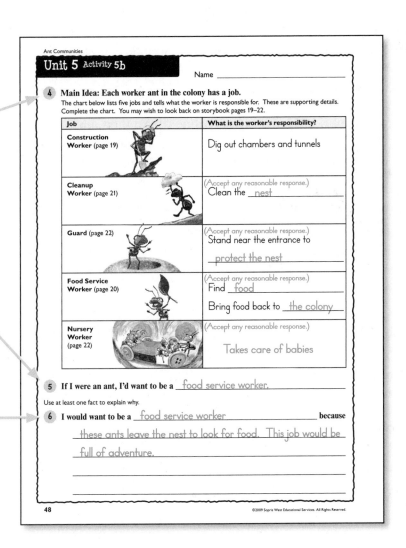

Ant Communities

Unit 5 Activity 5b

Name _____

4 Main Idea: Each worker ant in the colony has a job.

The chart below lists five jobs and tells what the worker is responsible for. These are supporting details.
Complete the chart. You may wish to look back on storybook pages 19–22.

Job	What is the worker's responsibility?
Construction Worker (page 19)	Dig out chambers and tunnels
Cleanup Worker (page 21)	(Accept any reasonable response.) Clean the _nest_
Guard (page 22)	(Accept any reasonable response.) Stand near the entrance to _protect the nest_
Food Service Worker (page 20)	(Accept any reasonable response.) Find _food_ Bring food back to _the colony_
Nursery Worker (page 22)	(Accept any reasonable response.) Takes care of babies

5 If I were an ant, I'd want to be a _food service worker._

Use at least one fact to explain why.

6 I would want to be a _food service worker_ because
these ants leave the nest to look for food. This job would be
full of adventure.
_____
_____

48 ©2009 Sopris West Educational Services. All Rights Reserved.

❶ SOUND REVIEW

Use selected Sound Cards from Units 1–5.

❷ SHIFTY WORD BLENDING

For each word, have students say the underlined sound. Then have them sound out the word smoothly and say it.

❸ ACCURACY AND FLUENCY BUILDING

- For each task, have students say any underlined part, then read the word.
- Set a pace. Then have students read the whole words in each task and column.
- Provide repeated practice, building accuracy first, then fluency.

B1. Reading by Analogy

Have students figure out how to say o-l by reading other words they know.

B2. Compound Words

- Remind students that compound words have two small words in one big word.
- For each word, have students figure out the compound word silently, then read the word.

C1. Multisyllabic Words

- For the list of words divided by syllables, have students read each syllable, then read the word. Use the word in a sentence, as appropriate.

buttons	I can't wear that shirt because I lost one of the . . . *buttons.*
purple	My favorite color is . . . *purple.*
dawdle	Go right home after school. Don't . . . *dawdle.*
marble	I saw something shiny in the grass. It was a . . . *marble.*
hospital	When Emma broke her arm, she went to the . . . *hospital.*

- For the list of whole words, build accuracy and then fluency.

E1. Tricky Words

- For each Tricky Word, have students use known sounds and word parts, then silently sound out the word. Use the word in a sentence to help with pronunciation.
- If the word is unfamiliar, tell students the word and have them say, spell, and say it.

treasures	The pirates searched for buried . . . *treasures.*

E2. Story Words

For each word, tell students the underlined sound and have them read the word.

imagination	The artist had a lot of . . . *imagination.*
accident	Brady was a reckless driver and got into an . . . *accident.*
dead	Something that is no longer alive is . . . *dead.*

❹ OPEN SYLLABLE O

Tell students the o in these words says its name.

❺ MORPHOGRAPHS

- Remind students that morphographs are word parts that mean something.
- Have students read "-ful = full of" and the related words and sentences.
- Have students rephrase each sentence.

An Ant With Ideas

Unit 5 Exercise 4
Use before Chapters 1 and 2

1. SOUND REVIEW Use selected Sound Cards from Units 1–5.

2. SHIFTY WORD BLENDING For each word, have students say the underlined part, sound out smoothly, then read the word.

bl<u>ew</u>	bl<u>ow</u>	<u>gr</u>ow	<u>gr</u>ow<u>n</u>	<u>gr</u>a<u>i</u>n

3. ACCURACY AND FLUENCY BUILDING For each column, have students say any underlined part, then read each word. Next, have students read the whole column.

A1 Sound Review	**B1** Reading by Analogy	**C1** Multisyllabic Words	**D1** Word Endings	**E1** Tricky Words
low	t<u>old</u>	but·tons	<u>marched</u>	treasures
throw	s<u>old</u>	pur·ple	<u>drinking</u>	color
slowed	r<u>oll</u>	daw·dle	<u>swirled</u>	world
		mar·ble	<u>ended</u>	eye
A2 Mixed Practice	**B2** Compound Words	hos·pi·tal	<u>attacked</u>	**E2** Story Words
t<u>igh</u>t	matchbox		<u>tunnels</u>	imagination
cra<u>ck</u>	leftover	buttons		acc<u>i</u>dent
<u>ea</u>sy	beside	purple	**D2** Bossy E	d<u>ea</u>d
wh<u>ee</u>ls	sunshine	dawdle	li<u>n</u>e	
	mouth-watering	marble	ma<u>d</u>e	
		hospital	li<u>k</u>ed	

4. OPEN SYLLABLE <u>O</u> Have students practice reading /ō/ and the related words.

o	m<u>o</u>·ment	An·t<u>o</u>·ni·a

5. MORPHOGRAPHS Have students practice reading "-ful = full of" and the related words and sentences.

(A)	-ful = full of	painful = full of pain	The cut on my arm was <u>painful</u>.
(B)		useful = full of use	The markers were very <u>useful</u>.
(B)	wonder<u>ful</u>	care<u>ful</u>	cheer<u>ful</u>

COMPREHENSION PROCESSES
Remember, Understand, Apply

PROCEDURES

1. Reviewing the Table of Contents

Identifying—Title; Using Table of Contents; Classifying—Genre

Using the Table of Contents on page 3 of the storybook, have students review the story title, genre, and chapter names. Say something like:

Turn to the Table of Contents on page 3.

Our next story begins on page 23.

What is the title of our next story? (An Ant With Ideas)

That's right. Look under the title.

Is this story fact or fiction? (fiction)

What does that mean?

(The story is make-believe. It's not real.)

Everyone, let's quickly read the chapter names.

(Chapter 1, Cleanup Worker; Chapter 2, Antonia's Ideas; Chapter 3, A Good Idea)

Turn to page 23.

2. Introducing the Story

Identifying—Title, Author; Viewing; Using Vocabulary—imagination; Inferring; Priming Background Knowledge; Predicting

Introduce the story "An Ant With Ideas" by discussing page 23 and the gray text questions.

Say something like:

What's the title of our story?

(An Ant With Ideas)

Who is the author? (Paula Rich)

Paula Rich has a great imagination. I think you will enjoy this story about an ant with ideas. Look at the picture.

What do you see in the picture that tells you that the story is fiction?

(The ants are wearing construction hats . . .)

We learned about construction ants. What facts do you remember about construction ants?

(They dig tunnels, make chambers . . .)

What do you think this story will be about?

(An ant that has ideas about construction . . .)

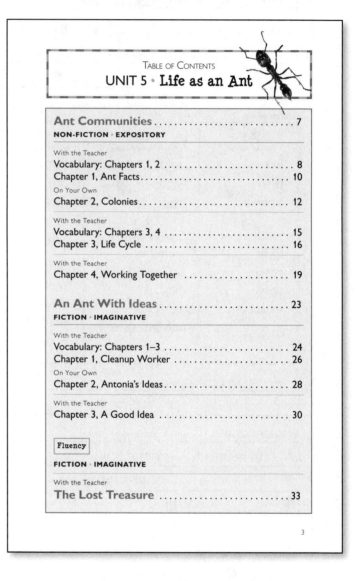

An Ant With Ideas

by Paula Rich

illustrated by David Opie

Look at the picture. Which ant do you think is the main character?**1** What makes you think the first ant is the main character?**2** What do you know about that ant already?**3**

23

COMPREHENDING
AS YOU GO

1 **Apply:** Inferring (The ant in front is the main character.)

2 **Apply:** Explaining (She is big and the other ants are looking at her.)

3 **Apply:** Inferring, Explaining (She is different from the others.)

COMPREHENSION PROCESSES

Understand, Apply

PROCEDURES

Introducing Vocabulary

> ☆imagination ☆treasure
> ☆dawdle ☆collapse
> ☆impressed

- For each vocabulary word, have students read the word by parts, then read the whole word.
- Read the student-friendly explanations to students as they follow with their fingers. Then have students use the vocabulary word by following the gray text.
- Review and discuss the photos and illustrations.

USING VOCABULARY

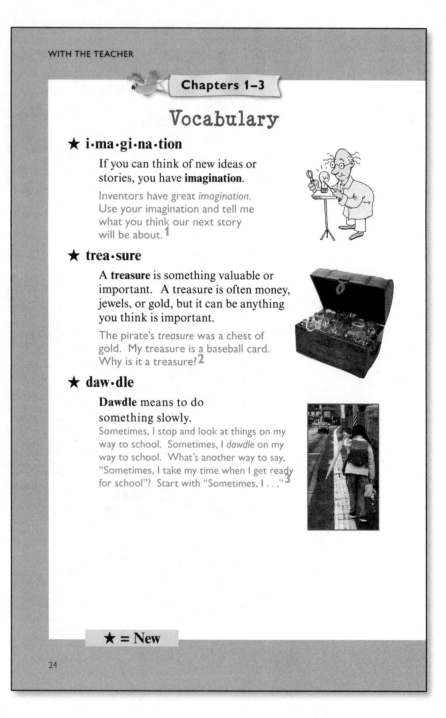

WITH THE TEACHER

Chapters 1–3

Vocabulary

★ **i·ma·gi·na·tion**

If you can think of new ideas or stories, you have **imagination**.

Inventors have great imagination. Use your imagination and tell me what you think our next story will be about.[1]

★ **trea·sure**

A **treasure** is something valuable or important. A treasure is often money, jewels, or gold, but it can be anything you think is important.

The pirate's treasure was a chest of gold. My treasure is a baseball card. Why is it a treasure?[2]

★ **daw·dle**

Dawdle means to do something slowly.

Sometimes, I stop and look at things on my way to school. Sometimes, I dawdle on my way to school. What's another way to say, "Sometimes, I take my time when I get ready for school"? Start with "Sometimes, I . . ."[3]

★ = New

24

① **Apply:** Predicting; Using Vocabulary—imagination (Maybe it will be about an ant who invents things. Maybe it will be about an ant with a lot of imagination . . .)

② **Apply:** Making Connections; Explaining; Using Vocabulary—treasure (Your baseball card is a treasure because baseball cards are important to you. Sometimes baseball cards are worth a lot of money, so they are a treasure . . .)

③ **Understand:** Using Vocabulary—dawdle (Sometimes I dawdle when I get ready for school.)

☆ = New in this unit

★ **col·lapse**

Collapse means to fall down suddenly and completely.

What's another way to say, "We built a tower of blocks, but it fell down"?[1]

★ **im·pressed**

To be **impressed** means to think someone does something really well.

Tim was *impressed* with Maria's new magic trick. What is something you are impressed with?[2]

Magic Show

25

USING VOCABULARY

[1] **Apply:** Making Connections; Using Vocabulary—collapse (We built a tower of blocks, but it kept collapsing.)

[2] **Understand:** Inferring; Using Vocabulary—impressed (I am impressed with our reading, my new bike, our new tetherball . . .)

CHAPTER 1 INSTRUCTIONS

Students read Chapter 1 with the teacher. Students read Chapter 2 on their own during independent work.

Note: If you're working on an 8- to 11-Day Plan, you will read Chapter 2 with students.

COMPREHENSION PROCESSES

Remember, Understand, Apply, Analyze, Evaluate

PROCEDURES

1. First Reading

- Ask questions and discuss the story as indicated by the gray text.
- Mix group and individual turns, independent of your voice.
  Have students work toward a group accuracy goal of 0–2 errors.
  Quietly keep track of errors made by all students in the group.
- After reading the story, practice any difficult words.
  Reread the story if students have not reached the accuracy goal.

2. Second Reading, Timed Readings: Repeated Reading

- As time allows, have students do Timed Readings while others follow along.
- Time individuals for 30 seconds and encourage each child to work for a personal best.
- Count the number of words read correctly in 30 seconds (words read minus errors). Multiply by two to determine words correct per minute. Record student scores.

WITH THE TEACHER

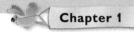

Chapter 1

Cleanup Worker

What kind of ant is this chapter going to be about? **1**

Antonia liked living next to the big red house. The grass was thick and green. The dirt was rich, black, and easy to dig. There were lots of mouth-watering insects to eat. But Antonia liked the trash cans best. Her nest was right beside them. Such wonderful things fell out of the cans! She found not only sweet food, but things that made her imagination fly.

Who is the main character? **2** Describe Antonia. **3**

26

FINGER TRACKING (Reminder)
To maintain attention and build fluency, continue having students track text with their fingers. Provide positive feedback and individual turns to students who are finger tracking.

COMPREHENDING AS YOU GO

❶ **Apply:** Predicting (a cleanup worker)

❷ **Remember:** Identifying—Main Character (Antonia is the main character.)

❸ **Understand:** Describing—Main Character (She is an ant with ideas. She lives next to a big red house. She likes to find treasures . . .)

AN ANT WITH IDEAS

Purple buttons, a matchbox, a drinking straw, marbles that swirled with color—why did the people in the big red house throw out such interesting things? Antonia kept her treasures in a deep crack in the sidewalk behind the cans.

Antonia was a cleanup worker. All day, she marched in a line with her sisters, taking leftover food out of the dark cool nest into the bright sunshine of the outside world. As they worked, she kept an eye out for more treasures around the trash cans. When she slowed down to look, her sisters would tell her, "Back to work, Antonia! No time to dawdle!"

What makes Antonia an interesting ant?**1** What are the things Antonia thinks are *treasures?* **2** Why do you think Antonia *dawdles?* **3**

27

COMPREHENDING
AS YOU GO

❶ **Analyze:** Drawing Conclusions; **Apply:** Using Vocabulary—treasure, imagination　(She likes to look for treasures. She has an imagination . . .)

❷ **Remember:** Identifying—What; Using Vocabulary—treasure　(Her treasures are things from the trash cans. Her treasures are buttons, marbles, a drinking straw, and a matchbox . . .)

❸ **Apply:** Inferring; Explaining; Using Vocabulary—dawdle　(She dawdles because she is looking for more treasures . . .)

CHAPTER 2 INSTRUCTIONS

Students read Chapter 2 on their own.

Note: If you're working on a lesson plan that is eight days or longer, you may be reading this chapter with your students.

COMPREHENSION PROCESSES

Remember, Understand, Apply, Evaluate

PROCEDURES

1. Getting Ready

Have students turn to "An Ant With Ideas," Chapter 2 on page 28. Tell students they are going to read on their own to the end of the chapter on page 29.

2. Setting a Purpose

Explaining, Making Judgments

Establish a purpose for reading. Say something like:

Look at page 28. What's the chapter title? (Antonia's Ideas)

Read to find out the answers to these questions:

- What were Antonia's ideas?
- Were Antonia's ideas good ideas or bad ideas?
- What did Antonia really want to do?

> **PREP NOTE**
>
> **Setting a Purpose**
>
> Write questions on a chalkboard, white board, or large piece of paper before working with your group.

3. Reading on Your Own: Partner or Whisper Reading

- Have students take turns reading every other page with a partner or have students whisper read pages 28–29 on their own.
- Continue having students track each word with their fingers.

4. Comprehension and Skill Work

Tell students that they will do Comprehension and Skill Activities 6 and 7 after they read on their own. Guide practice, as needed. See pages 64 and 65 of this guide.

5. Homework 4: Repeated Reading

 **Chapter 2**

Antonia's Ideas

All day long, Antonia helped her sisters clean the nest. But when the ants marched out into the world, Antonia kept her eye out for treasures near the trash cans.

Antonia liked her job as a cleanup worker, but she really wanted to be a construction worker. After all, an ant with ideas should be in construction!

One time, Antonia had an idea to put a pretty marble on top of their nest. She thought that if any other ants attacked their nest, she and her sisters could roll the marble down the nest hill to stop them. But the marble rolled off by accident one day, and 27 of her sisters ended up in the hospital.

How did Antonia think the marble could be used?[1] What was the problem?[2]
Why did Antonia think she should be a construction worker?[3]

28

COMPREHENDING AS YOU GO

❶ Understand: Explaining (She thought the ants could roll the marble down their anthill if other ants attacked their nest.)

❷ Understand: Explaining—Problem (The marble rolled off by accident and hurt some of her sister ants.)

❸ Apply: Explaining (She thought she should be a construction worker because she had lots of ideas.)

AN ANT WITH IDEAS

Then Antonia had an idea to put the purple buttons on the matchbox, like wheels on a cart. It would be useful for moving the baby ants around, she thought. But the matchbox cart got stuck in the tight turns of the nest's tunnels. And the baby ants got carsick.

"No more ideas!" her sisters said. "Back to work! No time to dawdle!"

Why didn't the matchbox cart work? **1** Do you think Antonia should stick to her job as a cleanup worker? Why or why not? **2**

29

COMPREHENDING
AS YOU GO

1 Understand: Explaining (The matchbox cart got stuck in the tunnels and made the baby ants carsick.)

2 Evaluate: Making Judgments (Yes, her ideas turn out to be bad ones. No, she should keep thinking of new things. Maybe a different idea will work out . . .)

★CHARACTERIZATION AND VOCABULARY

COMPREHENSION PROCESSES

Understand, Apply, Analyze

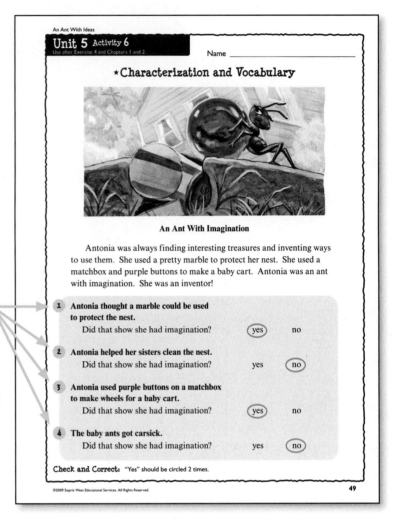

Inferring—Characterization
Drawing Conclusions
Using Vocabulary—imagination

PROCEDURES

For each step, demonstrate and guide practice, as needed. Then have students complete the page independently.

1. Paragraph Reading—Basic Instructions

Have students read the title and passage. Tell students that the passage describes how Antonia uses her imagination. Having an imagination is one of Antonia's character traits.

2. Selection Response—Specific Instructions (Items 1–4)

- Tell students that they will read sentences, then decide whether the sentence shows that Antonia had imagination.
- Have students read item 1. Guide students as they think about the answer. Say something like:

  Read item 1. (Antonia thought a marble could be used to protect the nest.
  Did that show she had imagination?)

  Let's think about that. Someone with imagination thinks of new ideas.
  Antonia thought a marble could be used to protect the nest.
  Is that a new idea about how to use a marble? (yes)
  So does that show us that Antonia had imagination? (yes)
  Yes, so we should circle the word yes. This shows that Antonia had imagination.

- Repeat with remaining items, as needed.

★ = New in this unit

STORY COMPREHENSION

COMPREHENSION PROCESSES

Understand, Apply

Using Graphic Organizer
Identifying—Setting; Describing

Using Graphic Organizer
Sequencing; Identifying—Goal,
Conclusion; Using Vocabulary—treasure

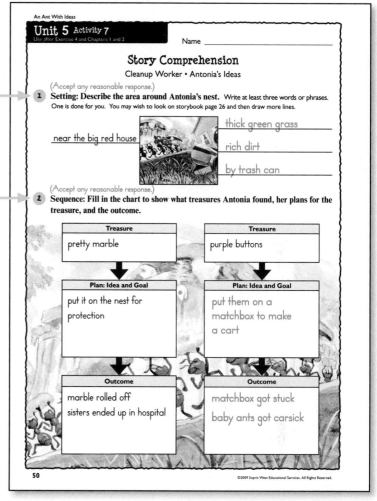

An Ant With Ideas

Unit 5 Activity 7
Use after Exercise 4 and Chapters 1 and 2

Name _____

Story Comprehension
Cleanup Worker • Antonia's Ideas

(Accept any reasonable response.)

1 Setting: Describe the area around Antonia's nest. Write at least three words or phrases. One is done for you. You may wish to look on storybook page 26 and then draw more lines.

near the big red house

thick green grass
rich dirt
by trash can

(Accept any reasonable response.)

2 Sequence: Fill in the chart to show what treasures Antonia found, her plans for the treasure, and the outcome.

Treasure	Treasure
pretty marble	purple buttons

Plan: Idea and Goal	Plan: Idea and Goal
put it on the nest for protection	put them on a matchbox to make a cart

Outcome	Outcome
marble rolled off sisters ended up in hospital	matchbox got stuck baby ants got carsick

50   ©2009 Sopris West Educational Services. All Rights Reserved.

PROCEDURES

For each step, demonstrate and guide practice, as needed. Then have students complete the page independently.

1. **Web/Setting—Specific Instructions** (Item 1)
   - Have students read the directions and brainstorm possible descriptions of the setting.
   - Have students write the answers in the blanks.

★ 2. **Sequence Chart—Introductory Instructions** (Item 2)
   - Have students read the directions and write answers in each box. Explain the relationship between the boxes by using the example provided. Say something like:

     Put your finger on the first column of boxes.
     Read the header in the first box. (Treasure)
     Read the header in the next box. (Plan: Idea and Goal)
     Read the header in the last box. (Outcome)

     The boxes from top to bottom tell the sequence of events—from the treasure to the plan and finally to the outcome. What is the treasure in the first box? (pretty marble)
     The arrow points to what Antonia planned to do with that marble.
     She planned to . . . (put it on the nest for protection).
     The arrow points to the outcome. What was the outcome?
     (The marble rolled off, and the sisters ended up in the hospital.)

   - Have students complete the boxes to tell the sequence of events with the purple buttons.

Self-monitoring
Have students check and correct their work.

① SOUND REVIEW

Have students read the sounds and key words in each row. Work for accuracy, then for fluency.

② ACCURACY AND FLUENCY BUILDING

- For each task, have students say any underlined part, then read the word.
- Set a pace. Then have students read the whole words in each task and column.
- Provide repeated practice, building accuracy first, then fluency.

B1. Shifty Words

- Tell students that one sound changes a word.
- Have students say the underlined sound, then read the word.

B2. Contractions

- Have students read "we have." Tell students the next word is a short way to say "we have." Then have students read the contraction.
- Repeat with "let's."

C1. Multisyllabic Words

For the list of words divided by syllables, have students read each syllable out loud, then read the word. Use the word in a sentence, as appropriate.

invention	The inventor came up with a new . . . *invention.*
tunnel	The worm dug a . . . *tunnel.*
sturdy	Ricardo built a fence that was strong and . . . *sturdy.*
colony	The group of ants lived in a . . . *colony.*
winter	It's cold in the . . . *winter.*

E1. Tricky Words

- For each Tricky Word, have students use known sounds and word parts, then silently sound out the word. Use the word in a sentence to help with pronunciation.
- If the word is unfamiliar, tell students the word and have them say, spell, and say it.

③ MORPHOGRAPHS AND AFFIXES

- Have students read the underlined part, then the word.
- For Row A, have students rephrase each word.
  What does restful mean? (full of rest) I had a restful evening! It was full of . . . rest.

④ WORDS IN CONTEXT

An Ant With Ideas

Unit 5 Exercise 5
Use before Chapter 3

1. SOUND REVIEW Have students review sounds for accuracy, then for fluency.

A	OW as in snow	u_e as in flute	ai as in rain	i_e as in kite	OO as in book
B	o_e	u	ew	igh	u_e

2. ACCURACY AND FLUENCY BUILDING For each column, have students say any underlined part, then read each word. Next, have students read the whole column.

A1 Mixed Practice	B1 Shifty Words	C1 Multisyllabic Words	D1 Word Endings	E1 Tricky Words
fl<u>ow</u>	dr<u>ew</u>	in•ven•tion	<u>strong</u>est	idea
<u>o</u>ver	dr<u>aw</u>	tun•nel	<u>zigg</u>ed	carried
cr<u>ew</u>	<u>str</u>aw	stur•dy	<u>zagg</u>ed	through
str<u>aw</u>	str<u>ay</u>	col•o•ny	<u>waggl</u>ed	**E2** Compound Words
pr<u>ou</u>d	**B2** Contractions	win•ter	cry	sidewalk
r<u>oo</u>f	we have		cried	behind
t<u>igh</u>t	we've	invention	use	cleanup
cra<u>ck</u>		tunnel	using	**E3** Story Words
<u>ea</u>sy	let us	sturdy		ex<u>c</u>ited
wh<u>ee</u>ls	let's	colony	collapse	sta<u>g</u>e
q<u>u</u>een		winter	collapsing	r<u>ea</u>dy
<u>z</u>one				

3. MORPHOGRAPHS AND AFFIXES Have students read the underlined word part, then the word.

A	rest<u>ful</u>	color<u>ful</u>	wonder<u>ful</u>	help<u>ful</u>
B	<u>ex</u>pect	<u>re</u>turn	sudden<u>ly</u>	<u>un</u>lit

4. WORDS IN CONTEXT Have students use the sounds and word parts they know and then the sentences to pronounce each underlined word.

A	pushed	To get out of the building, I <u>pushed</u> open the door.
B	trea•sure	The king gave her a beautiful ring from his <u>treasure</u> chest.

33

CHAPTER 3 INSTRUCTIONS
Students read Chapter 3 with the teacher.

COMPREHENSION PROCESSES
Understand, Apply, Evaluate

PROCEDURES

1. Reviewing Chapters 1, 2

Identifying—What; Making Judgments; Identifying—Goal
Review Chapters 1 and 2 by reviewing one or two events from each chapter.
Say something like: You read Chapter 2 on your own. Let's talk about what you read.
What were Antonia's ideas?
(She thought a marble could be used to protect the nest. She thought buttons and a matchbox could be made into a cart and used to move the babies around.)
Were Antonia's ideas good or bad? (They were good ideas, but they didn't work . . .)
What did Antonia really want to do? (She wanted to be a construction worker.)

2. First Reading
- Ask questions and discuss the story as indicated by the gray text.
- Mix group and individual turns, independent of your voice.
  Have students work toward a group accuracy goal of 0–2 errors.
  Quietly keep track of errors made by all students in the group.
- After reading the story, practice any difficult words.
  Repeat if students have not reached the accuracy goal.

3. Second Reading, Short Passage Practice: Developing Prosody
- Demonstrate expressive, fluent reading on the first paragraph. Read at a rate slightly faster than the students' rate. Say something like:
  Listen to my expression as I read the first paragraph. I'm going to pretend I'm telling you the story, so I want to make it sound as interesting as I can.

  "The Queen was going to start laying eggs very soon, and the ant colony needed a new nursery. The nursery had to be warm in the winter and cool in the summer . . . "

- Guide practice with your voice.
- Provide individual turns while others track with their fingers and whisper read.
  Provide descriptive and positive feedback.
- Repeat with one paragraph or one page at a time.

4. Partner or Whisper Reading: Repeated Reading
Before beginning independent work, have students finger track and do Partner or Whisper Reading.

5. Comprehension and Skill Work
Tell students they will do Comprehension and Skill Activities 8, 9a, and 9b after they read Chapter 3. Guide practice, as needed. For teacher directions, see pages 73–75.

6. Homework 5: Repeated Reading

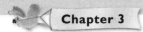
Chapter 3

A Good Idea

Describe some of Antonia's ideas.**1** What do you think is going to happen in this chapter?**2**

The Queen was going to start laying eggs very soon, and the ant colony needed a new nursery. The nursery had to be warm in the winter and cool in the summer. It had to be down deep in the ground.

Building the new nursery was a hard job for the construction workers. Dirt had to be carried a long way out of the nest. One of the tunnels kept collapsing.

Why are the construction workers building a new nursery?**3** What problems are they having?**4**

30

FINGER TRACKING (Reminder)
To maintain attention and build fluency, continue having students track text with their fingers. Provide positive feedback and individual turns to students who are finger tracking.

COMPREHENDING AS YOU GO

1 **Understand:** Describing (Antonia thought that a marble could roll down the nest hill to stop other ants that attacked their nest. She made a cart with purple buttons and a matchbox for moving the babies around.)

2 **Apply:** Predicting (Maybe Antonia will have more ideas. Maybe Antonia will become a construction worker . . .)

3 **Understand:** Explaining (They need a new nursery because the Queen will start laying eggs soon.)

4 **Apply:** Explaining—Problem; Using Vocabulary—collapse (They had to carry dirt a long way out of the nest. One of the tunnels kept collapsing.)

AN ANT WITH IDEAS

As the cleanup workers marched past the construction zone, Antonia had an idea. She stopped suddenly. The line of ants behind her zigged and zagged as her sisters ran into each other. They didn't like that.

"There's so much work to do!" they cried. Their antennas waggled up and down when they were excited. "Let's get going! We've got to clean the Queen's chamber, and the sleeping chambers, and the tunnels! No time to dawdle!"

But Antonia wanted to help the construction team. She had an idea! The drinking straw—it was sturdy and round. An ant could walk through it.

"How about using a straw to hold up the tunnel roof?" Antonia asked.

How did Antonia want to help the construction crew? **1** How could the straw help them with the tunnel that kept *collapsing*? **2**

31

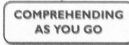

COMPREHENDING AS YOU GO

❶ Apply: Inferring, Explaining (She wanted to help them build a tunnel that did not collapse.)

❷ Apply: Inferring; Explaining; Using Vocabulary—collapsing (They could put the straw in the tunnel to keep the roof from collapsing. The straw could hold the roof up . . .)

WITH THE TEACHER

At first the construction workers laughed. But then the crew leader said, "Time's getting short! Let's try Antonia's idea."

So Antonia and 10 of the strongest workers got the straw from the crack in the sidewalk. They pushed and pulled it down to the collapsing tunnel. It worked! The tunnel roof stayed up.

The crew leader was impressed. Antonia's invention made the work go much faster. "An ant with ideas should be in construction!" the crew leader said. "Let's get to work, Antonia! No time to dawdle!"

Soon the Queen had a beautiful new nursery. Antonia was proud to be part of the construction team. She couldn't wait for their next job, because she had more treasures and more ideas to share!

Close your eyes. Imagine a straw in the ants' nest. How are the ants using the straw? **1** Why was the leader of the construction crew *impressed* with Antonia? **2**

32

COMPREHENDING AS YOU GO

1 **Understand:** Visualizing; Describing; Using Vocabulary—collapse (The ants dragged the straw down to where the tunnel was collapsing. They used the straw to hold up the roof . . .)

2 **Apply:** Inferring; Explaining; Using Vocabulary—impressed (The leader was impressed because Antonia's idea made the work go faster. Her idea kept the tunnel from collapsing.)

JUST FOR FUN • ANTONIA'S TREASURE

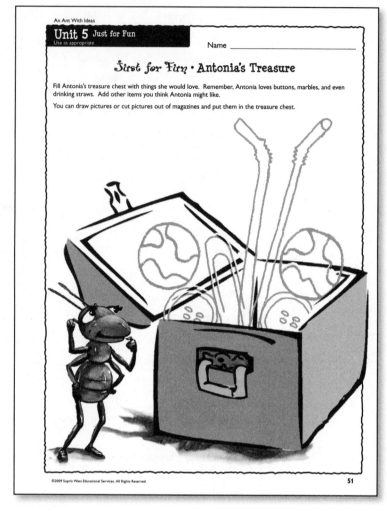

An Ant With Ideas

Unit 5 Just for Fun
Use as appropriate

Name _____

Just for Fun • Antonia's Treasure

Fill Antonia's treasure chest with things she would love. Remember, Antonia loves buttons, marbles, and even drinking straws. Add other items you think Antonia might like.

You can draw pictures or cut pictures out of magazines and put them in the treasure chest.

51

HOW TO USE "JUST FOR FUN" ACTIVITIES

Note: This activity is optional and is *just for fun.* Use the activity:
• as a cushion activity
• for homework
• just for fun

PROCEDURES

Illustrating—Specific Instructions

As time allows, have students draw items that Antonia would love. Students can draw pictures or cut out items from magazines to fill the treasure chest.

This page may be given to students as homework.

STORY MAP

COMPREHENSION PROCESSES
Remember, Understand, Apply

WRITING TRAITS
Conventions—Complete Sentence, Period

Using Graphic Organizer
Summarizing, Sequencing

Identifying—Setting

Describing—Main Character
Using Vocabulary—imagination

Explaining—Beginning, Goal

Explaining—Middle, Action
Using Vocabulary—protect

Explaining—End, Outcome/Conclusion

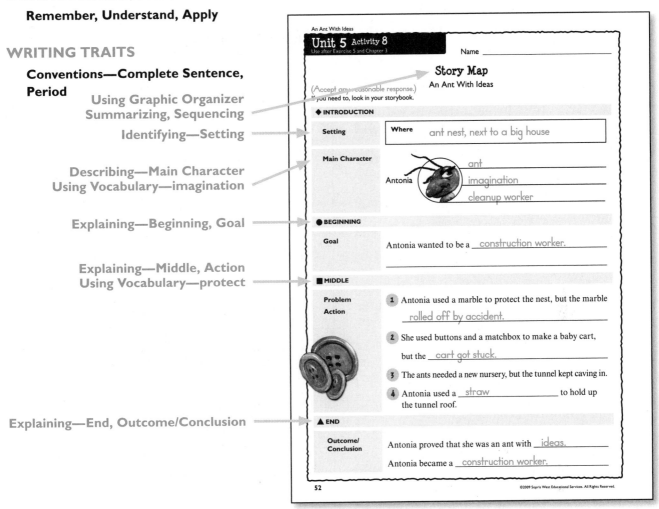

An Ant With Ideas

Unit 5 Activity 8
Use after Exercise 5 and Chapter 3

Name _____

Story Map
An Ant With Ideas

(Accept any reasonable response.)
If you need to, look in your storybook.

◆ INTRODUCTION

Setting — Where — ant nest, next to a big house

Main Character — Antonia — ant / imagination / cleanup worker

● BEGINNING

Goal — Antonia wanted to be a ___construction worker.___

■ MIDDLE

Problem Action
1. Antonia used a marble to protect the nest, but the marble ___rolled off by accident.___
2. She used buttons and a matchbox to make a baby cart, but the ___cart got stuck.___
3. The ants needed a new nursery, but the tunnel kept caving in.
4. Antonia used a ___straw___ to hold up the tunnel roof.

▲ END

Outcome/ Conclusion
Antonia proved that she was an ant with ___ideas.___
Antonia became a ___construction worker.___

52   ©2009 Sopris West Educational Services. All Rights Reserved.

PROCEDURES

Use an overhead BLM copy of the story map to demonstrate and guide practice, as needed.

Story Map—Basic Instructions

- Have students complete each section of the story map: setting, main character, beginning, middle, and end. Remind students to put a period at the end of a sentence.
- For some groups, provide students with time to complete each section before you move to the next.
- For more independent writers, demonstrate and guide how to complete the entire story map, then have students complete their own maps independently.

Self-monitoring

Have students check and correct their work.

COMING SOON!
Written Retells
In Comprehension and Skill Activities 9a and 9b, your students will use their story maps to write their first written retell. Be sure to tell students that doing a good job on their story map will help them be great writers.

★ WRITTEN RETELL

COMPREHENSION PROCESSES
Remember, Understand, Apply

WRITING TRAITS
Conventions—Complete Sentence, Beginning Capital, Period

Summarizing, Sequencing
Sentence Completion/Writing

Identifying—Setting, Main Character
Describing—Main Character

Explaining—Beginning, Goal

Explaining—Middle, Action

PROCEDURES
Use an overhead BLM copy of the story map to demonstrate and guide how to create a written retell.

☆ Written Retell—Introductory Instructions

1. Demonstrate and guide how to use the story map to write the introduction.

   We're going to use our story maps to write written retells.

   A written retell is a shortened version of the story that includes the setting, the main character, and the important actions or events in the story. A good written retell has an introduction, a beginning, a middle, and an end—just like the story does.

   First, we're going to complete the introduction.

   Look at my story map. Where did the story take place? (near an ants' nest, near a big red house)

   We're going to use that information to complete the introductory sentence.

   Put your finger on the diamond. Now we're going to write the introduction.

   Let's read and finish the sentence. (Antonia was a little ant who lived in an ants' nest next to a big red house.)

   So I'll write "in an ants' nest next to a big red house."

   Who is the main character? (Antonia) What does my story map say about her? (Antonia is an ant. She has imagination . . .)

   We're going to use that information to write a sentence or two that describes Antonia. We already said she was an ant.

   What could I write? (Antonia was an ant with imagination.)

   What else could we write? (She was an inventor.)

   That's a great introduction.

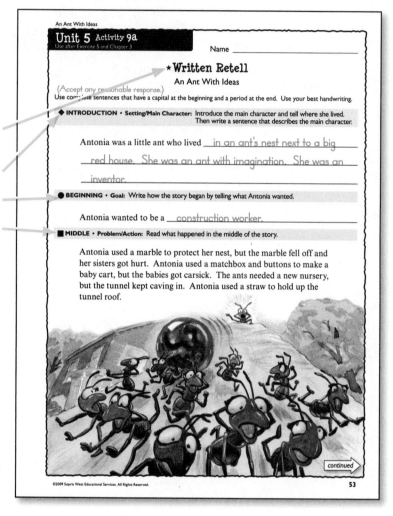

☆ = New in this unit

WRITTEN RETELL (*continued*)

Explaining—End, Outcome/Conclusion

Visualizing, Illustrating

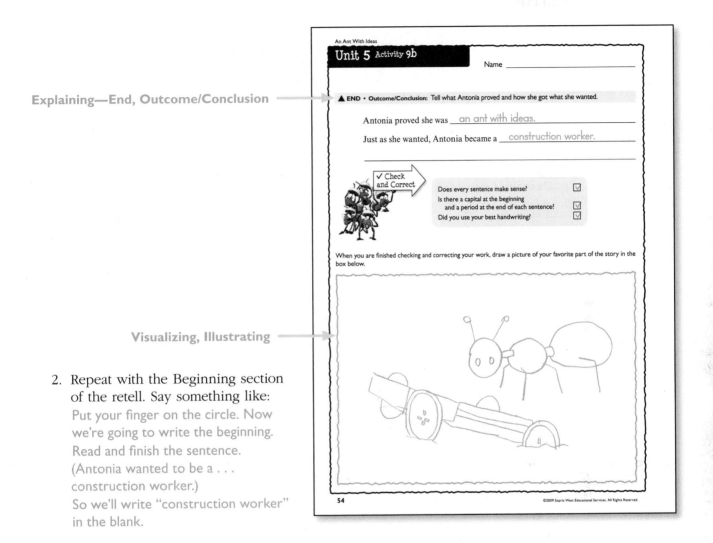

An Ant With Ideas

Unit 5 Activity 9b

Name _____

▲ END • Outcome/Conclusion: Tell what Antonia proved and how she got what she wanted.

Antonia proved she was ___an ant with ideas.___

Just as she wanted, Antonia became a ___construction worker.___

_____

✓ Check and Correct

Does every sentence make sense? ☑

Is there a capital at the beginning and a period at the end of each sentence? ☑

Did you use your best handwriting? ☑

When you are finished checking and correcting your work, draw a picture of your favorite part of the story in the box below.

54 ©2009 Sopris West Educational Services. All Rights Reserved.

2. Repeat with the Beginning section of the retell. Say something like:
   Put your finger on the circle. Now we're going to write the beginning.
   Read and finish the sentence.
   (Antonia wanted to be a . . . construction worker.)
   So we'll write "construction worker" in the blank.

3. Have students read the middle of the retell. Say something like:
   Put your finger on the square. The middle of the retell is done for us.
   Let's read about the things that happened in the middle of the story.
   Antonia used a marble to protect her . . .
   That was a good example of a retell. It told about the marble, the matchbox and buttons, and the straw. It also told how Antonia used each of those things.

4. Demonstrate and guide how to use the story map to write the end of the retell.
   Look at my story map. What happened in the end? (Antonia proved that she was an ant with ideas. Antonia became a construction worker.)
   Put your finger on the triangle. Read and finish the sentences.
   (Antonia proved she was . . . an ant with ideas.)
   So we'll write "an ant with ideas" in the blank.
   Read the next one with me. Just as she wanted, Antonia became a . . . construction worker.
   So what will we write in the blank? (construction worker)

   Have students check and correct their work, check the boxes, then illustrate their favorite part of the story.

① SOUND REVIEW
Use selected Sound Cards from Units 1–5.

② SOUND PRACTICE
- For each task, have students spell and say the focus sound in the gray bar. Next, have students read each underlined sound, the word, then the whole column.
- Repeat with each column, building accuracy first, then fluency.

③ ACCURACY AND FLUENCY BUILDING
- For each task, have students say any underlined part, then read the word.
- Set a pace. Then have students read the whole words in each task and column.
- Provide repeated practice, building accuracy first, then fluency.

<table>
<tr><td></td><td></td><td>**BUILD ACCURACY AND FLUENCY (Reminder)**</td></tr>
</table>

BUILD ACCURACY AND FLUENCY (Reminder)

For all rows and columns, follow the specific directions, then build accuracy and fluency with whole words.

Repeat rows and columns mixing group and individual turns, independent of your voice.

C1. Multisyllabic Words
For the list of words divided by syllables, have students read each syllable out loud, finger count the syllables, then read the word. Use the word in a sentence, as appropriate.

protect	2 syllables	Policemen serve and . . . *protect.*
nursery	3 syllables	Newborn babies stay in a hospital's . . . *nursery.*
finally	3 syllables	After many tries, I made a goal . . . *finally.*
tunnels	2 syllables	Anthills have many . . . *tunnels.*
antennas	3 syllables	Some insects have . . . *antennas.*
underneath	3 syllables	I couldn't see the bug on top of the log, so I looked . . . *underneath.*

D1. Tricky Words
- For each Tricky Word, have students use known sounds and word parts, then silently sound out the word. Use the word in a sentence to help with pronunciation.
- If the word is unfamiliar, tell students the word and have them say, spell, and say it.

④ MORPHOGRAPHS AND AFFIXES
- Have students read the underlined part, then the word.
- Repeat practice with whole words, mixing group and individual turns. Build accuracy, then fluency.

Fluency

Unit 5 Exercise 6
Use before The Lost Treasure

1. SOUND REVIEW Use selected Sound Cards from Units 1–5.

2. SOUND PRACTICE In each column, have students spell and say the sound, then say any underlined sound and the word. Next, have students read the whole column.

ow as in snow	o as in open	aw	ue, ew
sn<u>ow</u>	<u>o</u>pen	cr<u>aw</u>led	gl<u>ue</u>
gr<u>ow</u>n	<u>o</u>ver	<u>aw</u>ful	cr<u>ew</u>
sh<u>ow</u>	m<u>o</u>tion	sees<u>aw</u>	bl<u>ue</u>s

3. ACCURACY AND FLUENCY BUILDING For each column, have students say any underlined part, then read each word. Next, have students read the whole column.

A1 Mixed Review	B1 Word Endings	C1 Multisyllabic Words		D1 Tricky Words
smell	<u>sleep</u>ing	pro·tect	protect	thought
small	<u>wiggl</u>ed	nurs·er·y	nursery	treasure
new	<u>stopp</u>ed	fin·al·ly	finally	every
now	**B2** Compound Words	tun·nels	tunnels	chamber
stuck	everywhere	an·ten·nas	antennas	**D2** Story Words
stick	inside	un·der·neath	underneath	stora<u>ge</u>
ever	hatpin			<u>hea</u>d
				n<u>ice</u>

4. MORPHOGRAPHS AND AFFIXES Have students read the underlined word part, then the word.

<u>re</u>fill	<u>ex</u>actly	fic<u>tion</u>	respect<u>ful</u>

FLUENCY PASSAGE INSTRUCTIONS

This Story Reading targets fluency as the primary goal of instruction and practice. Students do repeated readings of this short passage to improve accuracy, expression, and rate.

COMPREHENSION PROCESSES

Understand, Analyze, Evaluate

PROCEDURES

1. Warm-Up: Partner or Whisper Reading

Before beginning group Story Reading, have students finger track and partner or whisper read the selection.

2. First Reading

- Ask questions as indicated by the gray text.
- Mix group and individual turns, independent of your voice.
  Have students work toward a group accuracy goal of 0–2 errors.
  Quietly keep track of errors made by all students in the group.
- After reading the story, practice any difficult words.
  Reread the story if students have not reached the accuracy goal.

CHECKOUT OPPORTUNITY

While students are Partner Reading, listen to individuals read the passage. Work on accuracy and fluency, as needed.

3. Second Reading, Short Passage Practice: Developing Prosody

- Demonstrate reading the first paragraph with expression and fluency. Have students finger track as you read.
- Have students choral read the first paragraph. Encourage reading with expression and fluency.
- Repeat with the second paragraph.

4. Third Reading, Group Timed Readings: Repeated Reading

- Encourage each child to work for a personal best. Have students whisper read for a one-minute Timed Reading. Tell students to go back to the top of the page and keep reading until the minute is up.
- Have students put their finger on the last word they read and count the number of words read correctly in one minute.
- Have students do a second Timed Reading of the same page.
- Have students try to beat their last score.
- Celebrate improvements.

5. Written Assessment (Comprehension and Skill)

Tell students they will do a Written Assessment after they read "The Lost Treasure." For teacher directions, see pages 80 and 81 in this guide.

6. Homework 6: Repeated Reading

WITH THE TEACHER

Fluency

The Lost Treasure

by Paula Rich
illustrated by David Opie

Antonia's new treasure was lost. She 　6
looked everywhere for it. She ran down all the 　15
tunnels of the nest. She stopped at every room 　24
and stuck her head inside. She wiggled her 　32
antennas to pick up a smell. It wasn't in the 　42
food storage rooms or in the sleeping chambers. 　50
She didn't see or smell it in any of the nurseries. 　61
She went into the hospital and crawled 　68
underneath all the beds. She even looked in the 　77
trash chambers—yuck! 　80

Finally, Antonia 　82
came to the Queen's 　86
chamber. There it was— 　90
the dark blue hatpin! 　94
The Queen thought it 　98
was beautiful. Antonia 　101
was happy to give her 　106
treasure to the Queen. 　110

At the beginning of the story, how did Antonia feel?[1] How could you tell?[2]
What did she do to solve her problem?[3] Do you think Antonia may have felt
bittersweet at the end? If so, why?[4]

33

FINGER TRACKING
(Reminder)
To maintain attention and build fluency, continue having students track text with their fingers. Provide positive feedback and individual turns to students who are finger tracking.

COMPREHENDING AS YOU GO

[1] **Analyze:** Inferring (She was worried. She was sad . . .)

[2] **Analyze:** Inferring; **Understand:** Explaining (She was looking all over for her new treasure.)

[3] **Remember:** Identifying—Action (She kept looking from room to room until she found her treasure.)

[4] **Evaluate:** Making Judgments; **Understand:** Explaining; Using Vocabulary—bittersweet (Yes, she was probably sad and glad. She probably wanted to keep the treasure for herself, but she was happy to give it to the Queen.)

★WRITTEN ASSESSMENT (1 of 2)

COMPREHENSION PROCESSES
Remember, Understand, Apply

WRITING TRAITS
**Conventions—Complete Sentence,
Beginning Capital, Period**

Test Taking

Identifying—Main Character
Sentence Completion

Identifying—Goal
Sentence Completion

Identifying—Problem

PROCEDURES
Do not demonstrate or guide practice.
**★Written Assessment—Introductory
Instructions**

Unit 5 Written Assessment
Use after Exercise 6 and The Lost Treasure

Beth, Another Ant With Imagination

Beth wanted to be a construction worker like her sister Antonia. Antonia was an ant with ideas. Beth had ideas too.

One winter day, the wind started to blow. Then it began to snow. The ants had a problem. The nest was growing colder. The ants were afraid that the nest was getting too cold for the baby ants. The ants were worried.

Then Beth remembered the colorful marble that lay near the nest. She said, "Remember that marble? We can use the marble to keep the nest warm. We can use it like a door. When the wind blows, we can push it in front of the hole to our nest.

"It will keep the snow out. Then the baby ants will survive."

The ants were impressed. Beth had great ideas! The ants said, "Beth, you should be a construction worker." Beth just smiled.

MAIN CHARACTER (1 point) (Accept any reasonable response.)
1 Who is the story about?

   The story is about ___an ant named Beth.___

GOAL (1 point) (Accept any reasonable response.)
2 At the beginning, what did Beth want?

   Beth wanted to be a ___construction worker.___

PROBLEM (1 point)
3 What was the ant colony's problem?
   ○ They didn't have enough food.
   ○ They had no ideas.
   ● The nest was getting too cold for the babies.

80

---

1. Introduce the Written Assessment.
   - Tell students that their work today is an opportunity for them to show what they can do independently. Say something like:
     We have been working really hard together, and you have learned many new skills and strategies. I'm very proud of you. Today, you get to show me what you can do all by yourself.

   - Tell students they will whisper read the passage and then answer the questions without help.
     You're going to whisper read a passage and then answer the questions—just like you've been doing on your Comprehension and Skill Work. The only thing that is different is you need to work by yourself.

     If you read a question and aren't sure what to do, reread the question and try again.
     What should you do if you can't answer a question? (Reread the question and try again.)
     If you still can't answer the question, reread the passage and try again.
     What should you do if you still can't answer a question?
     (Reread the passage and try again.)
     If you still aren't sure, just do your best and keep going.

 = New in this unit

Inferring, Explaining

Explaining—Solution

Defining Vocabulary—impressed

Describing—Main Character
(characterization)
Sentence Writing

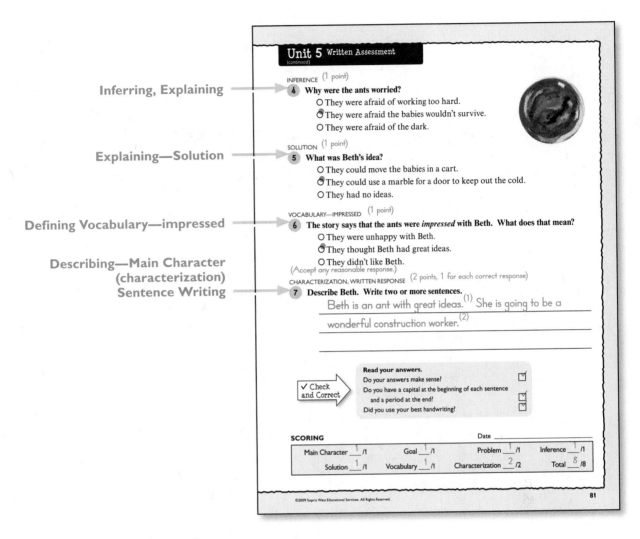

Unit 5 Written Assessment
(continued)

INFERENCE (1 point)

4 **Why were the ants worried?**
○ They were afraid of working too hard.
◐ They were afraid the babies wouldn't survive.
○ They were afraid of the dark.

SOLUTION (1 point)

5 **What was Beth's idea?**
○ They could move the babies in a cart.
◐ They could use a marble for a door to keep out the cold.
○ They had no ideas.

VOCABULARY—IMPRESSED (1 point)

6 **The story says that the ants were** *impressed* **with Beth. What does that mean?**
○ They were unhappy with Beth.
◐ They thought Beth had great ideas.
○ They didn't like Beth.

(Accept any reasonable response.)

CHARACTERIZATION, WRITTEN RESPONSE (2 points, 1 for each correct response)

7 **Describe Beth. Write two or more sentences.**

Beth is an ant with great ideas.(1) She is going to be a

wonderful construction worker.(2)

_____

✓ Check and Correct

Read your answers.
Do your answers make sense?
Do you have a capital at the beginning of each sentence
and a period at the end?
Did you use your best handwriting?

SCORING   Date _____

| Main Character __1__/1 | Goal __1__/1 | Problem __1__/1 | Inference __1__/1 |
| Solution __1__/1 | Vocabulary __1__/1 | Characterization __2__/2 | Total __8__/8 |

81

2. Check for student understanding.
   Say something like:
   Look at your assessment. What are you going to do first? (write my name)
   What are going to do next? (whisper read the passage)
   What will you do after you read the passage? (answer the questions)

   That's great. Now what will you do if you get to a hard question?
   (reread the question and try again)
   That's right. What should you do if it's still hard? (reread the passage and try again)
   Very good. And if you still aren't sure, what will you do? (do my best and keep going)

3. Remind students to check and correct.
   When you finish your assessment, what should you do? (check and correct)
   That's right. Go to the top of the page. Reread the questions and make sure your answers
   make sense. Fix anything that doesn't sound right. Make sure you have an answer for
   every question.

4. Remind students what to do when they finish their work.

End of the Unit

In this section, you will find:

Making Decisions

As you near the end of the unit, plan to give the Written Assessment and the Oral Reading Fluency Assessment to each child in your group. Use this section as a general guide for making instructional decisions and doing diagnostic planning.

Written Assessment

The Unit 5 Written Assessment is located on page 80 of the students' *Activity Book 1* and on the CD.

Oral Reading Fluency Assessment

The Unit 5 Oral Reading Fluency Assessment is located on page 86 and in the *Assessment Manual*.

Certificate of Achievement and Goal Setting

Celebrate your children's accomplishments. When your students master the unit skills, send home the Certificate of Achievement. Have students set goals for the next unit.

Extra Practice Lessons

Use the Extra Practice lessons for students who need additional decoding and fluency work. Student materials can be copied from the Extra Practice blackline masters.

Making Decisions

GENERAL ASSESSMENT GUIDELINES

1. After students read Story Reading 6, "The Lost Treasure," give the group the Unit 5 Written Assessment in place of Comprehension and Skill Work. Follow the instructions on pages 80 and 81 of this guide.

2. While the group is completing the Written Assessment, or any time during the day, administer the Oral Reading Fluency Assessment. Assess each student individually.

3. Score oral fluency responses on the Student Assessment Record. Adhere to the scoring criteria in the *Assessment Manual*. Use a stopwatch to time how long it takes each student to read the Oral Reading Fluency Passage and record errors.

USING THE WRITTEN ASSESSMENT RESULTS

Results of the Written Assessment *should not* be used to determine whether a student or group of students continues forward in the program. As long as students pass the Oral Reading Fluency Assessment, they should continue forward with the next unit.

The Written Assessment should be used to informally monitor how well students read independently and answer questions in writing. If any student has difficulty with the Written Assessment, re-administer the assessment orally.

If the student has difficulty answering the questions orally:
- Record the types of errors (e.g., main idea, sequencing, open-ended response).
- Provide explicit instruction for these types of questions during reading group, before independent work, and in tutorials, as needed.
  1. Demonstrate (or model) appropriate responses, guide practice, and provide opportunities for independent practice.
  2. For inferential questions, think aloud with students—explain how you arrive at an answer.
  3. For literal questions, teach students to reread a passage, locate information, reread the question, and respond.

At this level, if the student is able to answer the questions orally but not on paper, it may not be due to comprehension problems. The student's difficulties may be related to a lack of motivation; an inability to work independently; or a struggle with handwriting, spelling, language, or vocabulary.

At the end of each unit, you will need to make decisions regarding student progress. Should students go forward in the program? Does the group need Extra Practice before proceeding?

Do individuals require more assistance and practice to continue working in their group? These decisions all require use of the oral reading fluency data and professional judgment. As you analyze assessment results, watch for trends and anomalies.

See the *Assessment Manual* for detailed information and instructional recommendations. General guidelines and recommendations follow:

Strong Pass ≥ 103 WCPM 0–2 errors	• Continue with the current pace of instruction. • Have students set goals. (Until students are reading approximately 180 words correct per minute, oral reading fluency continues to be an instructional goal.)
Pass 82–102 WCPM 0–2 errors	• Continue with the current pace of instruction. Consider increasing fluency practice.
No Pass ≤ 81 WCPM	• If a child scores a No Pass but has previously passed all assessments, you may wish to advance the student to the next unit, then carefully monitor the student. • If a child scores a No Pass but has previously passed all assessments, you may wish to advance the student to the next unit and also provide additional practice opportunities. (See below.) • If a child scores two consecutive No Passes or periodic No Passes, additional practice must be provided. (See below.) • If a child scores three consecutive No Passes, the student should be placed in a lower-performing group.

> **RED FLAG**
> A No Pass is a red flag. A mild early intervention can prevent an intense and time-consuming intervention in the future.

Added Practice Options for Groups

Warm-Ups: Begin each story reading with a review of the previous day's story. After reading the story, include Short Passage Practice on a daily basis.

Extended Units: If several children begin to score No Passes or barely pass, consider extending the unit by adding Extra Practice Lessons 1, 2, and/or 3. Extra Practice lessons include Decoding Practice, Fluency Passage, Word Fluency, and an Activity. (See pages 88 to 99 in this guide.)

Vowel Review: Consider a review of selected vowel units from *Read Well 1* or *Fluency Foundations*.

Added Practice Options for Individual Students

Tutorials: Set up five-minute tutorials on a daily basis with an assistant, trained volunteer, or cross-age tutor. Have the tutor provide Short Passage Practice and Timed Readings or Extra Practice lessons.

Double Dose: Find ways to provide a double dose of *Read Well* instruction:
• Have the student work in his or her group *and* a lower-performing group.
• Have an instructional assistant, older student, or parent volunteer preview or review lessons.
• Have an instructional assistant provide instruction with Extra Practice lessons.

END-OF-THE-UNIT CELEBRATION

When students pass the Oral Reading Fluency Assessment, celebrate with the Certificate of Achievement on page 87.

Note: Using the Flesch-Kincaid Grade Level readability formula, the Unit 5 Assessment has a 2.2 readability level. Readabilities are based on number of words per sentence and number of syllables per word. Adding one or two multisyllabic words can increase readability by a month or two. Though we are attending to readability for the assessments, the overriding factor is decodability.

GOAL SETTING

If you choose to do goal setting with students, help them brainstorm accomplishments in reading.

Say something like:

Let's look at our goal-setting form.
It starts with "I am proud because I can . . ."

I'm proud of you because you can read nonfiction.
I'm also proud of you because you can read with expression. What are you proud of?
(beating my last fluency score . . .)

That's a great accomplishment.
It is something to be proud of!
Please complete the sentence, "I am proud because I can . . ."

The next line says, "My goal is to . . ."
For Unit 6, I'd like all of you to work on increasing your reading fluency by one word per minute. What does your goal say? (My goal is to read one word per minute faster.)

The next line says, "To reach my goal, I will . . ."
Everyone, read the dots. What will you do to reach your goal?
(do my best in reading group, read and reread my stories . . .)

[Jason], what will you do to improve your reading fluency? (read my homework)

The next part of your form tells you what your fluency was for Unit 5. It also tells you what your personal best is. Please whisper read the sentence that begins, "In this unit . . ."
I think everyone is going to meet their goals for Unit 6!

TRICKY WORD and *FOCUS SKILL WARM-UP*

would	work	know	communities	guard	useful

ORAL READING FLUENCY PASSAGE

Ant Colonies

★Did you know that ants live and work together? Just like people, these amazing animals live and work together in communities. | 10
| 20
| 21

Think about it. If you were an ant, you would be very useful. You would have an important job. You might guard the nest or take care of the baby ants. You might be a cleanup worker or gather food. Ants are very strong. If you were an ant, you would drag big chunks of food back to the nest. | 33
| 44
| 58
| 71
| 81

You might even grow up to be a queen. If you were the queen, you would have your own room. You would lay thousands and thousands of eggs. You would have a wonderful life. All the other ants would wait on you! If you were an ant, what job would you want? | 94
| 105
| 117
| 131
| 133

ORAL READING FLUENCY	Start timing at the ★. Mark errors. Make a single slash in the text (/) at 60 seconds. Have the student complete the passage. If the student completes the passage in less than 60 seconds, have the student go back to the ★ and continue reading. Make a double slash (//) in the text at 60 seconds.
WCPM	Determine words correct per minute by subtracting errors from words read in 60 seconds.
STRONG PASS	The student scores no more than 2 errors on the first pass through the passage and reads 103 or more words correct per minute. Proceed to Unit 6.
PASS	The student scores no more than 2 errors on the first pass through the passage and reads 82 to 102 words correct per minute. Proceed to Unit 6.
NO PASS	The student scores 3 or more errors on the first pass through the passage and/or reads 81 or fewer words correct per minute. Provide added fluency practice with *RW2* Unit 5 Extra Practice. (Lessons follow the certificate at the end of the teacher's guide.) After completing the Extra Practice, retest the student.

Congratulations!

_____

has successfully completed

Read Well 2 Unit 5 • *Life as an Ant*

with _____ words correct per minute.

Teacher Signature _____

Date _____

Goal Setting

I am proud because I can _____ .

My goal is to read one word per minute faster.

To reach my goal, I will:

- Do my best in reading group.
- Read and reread my stories.
- Read my homework.

Signed _____

Date _____

My Personal Best:

In this unit, my fluency was _____ .

My personal best is _____ words correct per minute.

PROCEDURES

1. Sound Review

Use selected Sound Cards from Units 1–5.

- Have students say each sound, building accuracy first, then fluency.
- Mix group and individual turns, independent of your voice.

2. Sounding Out Smoothly

- For each word, have students say the underlined part, sound out the word smoothly, then read the whole word. Use the words in sentences, as needed.
- Have students read all the words in the row, building accuracy first, then fluency.
- Repeat practice. Mix group and individual turns, independent of your voice.

3. Accuracy and Fluency Building

- For each task, have students say any underlined part, then read each word.
- Set a pace. Then have students read the whole words in each task and column.
- Provide repeated practice, building accuracy first, then fluency.

4. Tricky Words

Have students read each row for accuracy, then read the entire grid for fluency.

5. Multisyllabic Words

For each word, have students read each syllable out loud, finger count the syllables, then tell how many syllables are in the word. If needed, use the word in a sentence. Have students read the whole word.

6. Dictation

back, pack, pick, trash, crash, splash

- Say "back." Have students say the word. Guide students as they finger count and say the sounds. Have students touch or write the sounds, then read the word. Say something like:

  The first word is *back.* Say the word. (back)

  Say and count the sounds in *back* with me.

  Hold up one finger for each sound. /b/•/ăăă/•/k/ How many sounds? (three)

  What's the first sound? (/b/) Touch under /b/.

  What's the next sound? (/ăăă/) Write /ăăă/.

  What's the last sound? (/k/) Touch under /k/.

  Read the word. (back)

- Repeat with "pack" and "pick."
- Continue with the rhyming words: trash, crash, splash.

Unit 5 Decoding Practice

Name _____

1. SOUND REVIEW Use selected Sound Cards from Units 1–5.

2. SOUNDING OUT SMOOTHLY Have students say the underlined part, sound out and read each word, then read the row.

n<u>ew</u>	s<u>aw</u>	<u>a</u>nt	j<u>o</u>b

3. ACCURACY/FLUENCY BUILDING Have students say any underlined part, then read each word. Next, have students read the column.

A1 Sound Practice	**B1** Word Endings	**C1** Rhyming Words	**D1** Buildups
<u>ow</u>n	car<u>eful</u>	m<u>igh</u>t	port
gr<u>ow</u>	us<u>eful</u>	r<u>igh</u>t	import
kn<u>ow</u>	late	br<u>igh</u>t	import<u>a</u>nt
m<u>o</u>st	later	**C2** Bossy E	**D2** Mixed Review
b<u>o</u>th	baby	s<u>a</u>me	ch<u>oo</u>se
A2 Compound Words	babies	t<u>a</u>ke	t<u>ow</u>ns
everyone	colony	t<u>i</u>me	m<u>o</u>re
something	colonies	l<u>i</u>fe	st<u>ar</u>t
inside			
outside			

4. TRICKY WORDS Have students read each row for accuracy, then fluency.

live	have	done	their	want	5
worker	build	people	one	change	10

5. MULTISYLLABIC WORDS Have students read the word by parts, tell how many syllables are in the word, then read the whole word.

Ⓐ	col•lect	collect	pro•tect	protect
Ⓑ	sur•vive	survive	dif•fer•ent	different
Ⓒ	com•mu•ni•ty	community	com•mu•ni•ties	communities

6. DICTATION Say the word. Have students say the word, then finger count and say the sounds. Have students say each sound as they touch or write it.

A1 Shifty Words	**B1** Rhyming Words
b <u>a</u> ck	t r <u>a s h</u>
<u>p</u> a ck	c r <u>a s h</u>
p <u>i</u> ck	s p l <u>a s h</u>

28

PROCEDURES

1. First Reading

Mix group and individual turns, independent of your voice. Have students work toward an accuracy goal of 0–2 errors and practice any difficult words.

2. Second Reading, Short Passage Practice: Developing Prosody

- Demonstrate how to read a line or two with expression. Read at a rate slightly faster than the students' rate. Say something like:

Listen as I read the first two sentences with expression and phrasing. I'm going to emphasize certain words and pause between sentences.

"Ants and people live, grow, and work in communities. People live in towns and have jobs that need to be done."

- Guide practice with your voice.
Now read the paragraph with me.

- Provide individual turns while others track with their fingers and whisper read. Provide descriptive, positive feedback.

[Joy], you read with wonderful expression!

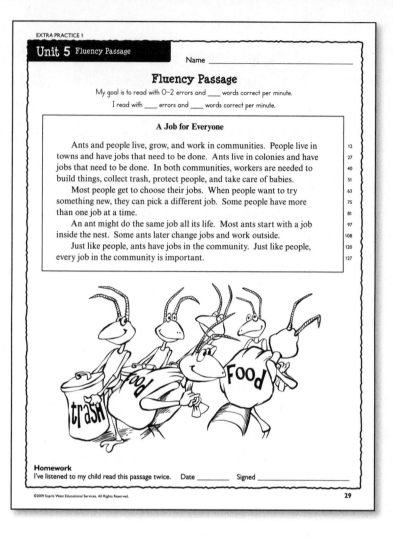

EXTRA PRACTICE 1

Unit 5 Fluency Passage

Name _____

Fluency Passage

My goal is to read with 0–2 errors and ____ words correct per minute.

I read with ____ errors and ____ words correct per minute.

A Job for Everyone

Ants and people live, grow, and work in communities. People live in towns and have jobs that need to be done. Ants live in colonies and have jobs that need to be done. In both communities, workers are needed to build things, collect trash, protect people, and take care of babies.

Most people get to choose their jobs. When people want to try something new, they can pick a different job. Some people have more than one job at a time.

An ant might do the same job all its life. Most ants start with a job inside the nest. Some ants later change jobs and work outside.

Just like people, ants have jobs in the community. Just like people, every job in the community is important.

| 12 |
| 27 |
| 40 |
| 51 |
| 63 |
| 75 |
| 81 |
| 97 |
| 108 |
| 120 |
| 127 |

Homework
I've listened to my child read this passage twice. Date _____ Signed _____

©2009 Sopris West Educational Services. All Rights Reserved.   **29**

3. Partner Reading: Repeated Reading (Checkout Opportunity)

While students are doing Partner Reading, listen to individuals read the passage. Work on accuracy and fluency, as needed.

4. Homework: Repeated Reading

Have students read the story at home.

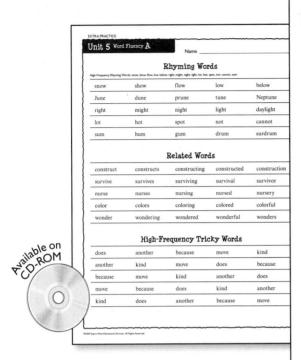

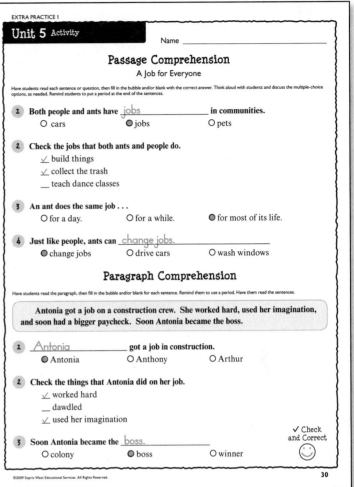

PROCEDURES

For each step, demonstrate and guide practice, as needed. Then have students complete the page independently.

1. Activity

Passage Comprehension

- Have students read each sentence or phrase, then fill in the bubble and blank or check the blank with the correct answer.
- Think aloud with students and discuss the multiple-choice options, as needed.
- Remind students to put a period at the end of sentences.

Paragraph Comprehension

- Have students read the paragraph.
- Have students read each numbered sentence or phrase, then fill in the bubble and blank or check the blank with the correct answer. Remind them to end sentences with a period, where needed.
- Have students read the completed sentences.

Self-monitoring

Have students read and check their work, then draw a happy face in the Check and Correct circle.

2. Word Fluency (BLMs are located on the CD.)

- To build fluency, have students read Rhyming Words, Related Words, and High-Frequency Tricky Words. Have students read each section three times in a row.
- To build accuracy, have students read all sets with partners.

> **ACCURACY BEFORE FLUENCY**
> **(Reminder)**
> Word Fluency is designed to build accuracy and fluency. Students should practice for accuracy before working on fluency.

PROCEDURES

1. Sound Review

Use selected Sound Cards from Units 1–5.
- Have students say each sound, building accuracy first, then fluency.
- Mix group and individual turns, independent of your voice.

2. Sounding Out Smoothly

- For each word, have students say the underlined part, sound out the word smoothly, then read the whole word. Use the words in sentences, as needed.
- Have students read all the words in the row, building accuracy first, then fluency.
- Repeat practice. Mix group and individual turns, independent of your voice.

3. Accuracy and Fluency Building

- For each task, have students say any underlined part, then read each word.
- Set a pace. Then have students read the whole words in each task and column.
- Provide repeated practice, building accuracy first, then fluency.

4. Tricky Words

Have students read each row for accuracy, then read the entire grid for fluency.

5. Multisyllabic Words

For each word, have students read each syllable out loud, finger count the syllables, then tell how many syllables are in the word. If needed, use the word in a sentence. Have students read the whole word.

6. Dictation

and, sand, thousand, cake, take, make

- Say "and." Have students say the word. Guide students as they finger count and say the sounds. Have students touch or write the sounds, then read the word.

  The first word is *and.* Say the word. (and)

  Say and count the sounds in *and* with me.

  Hold up one finger for each sound. /ăăă/•/nnn/•/d/ How many sounds? (three)

  What's the first sound? (/ăăă/) Write /ăăă/.

  What's the next sound? (/nnn/) Touch under /nnn/.

  What's the last sound? (/d/) Touch under /d/.

  Read the word. (and)

- Repeat with "sand" and "thousand."
- Continue with the rhyming words: cake, take, make.

EXTRA PRACTICE 2

Unit 5 Decoding Practice

Name _____

1. SOUND REVIEW Use selected Sound Cards from Units 1–5.

2. SOUNDING OUT SMOOTHLY Have students say the underlined part, sound out and read each word, then read the row.

| gl<u>a</u>d | n<u>e</u>st | p<u>ea</u>ch | j<u>u</u>st |

3. ACCURACY/FLUENCY BUILDING Have students say any underlined part, then read each word. Next, have students read the column.

A1 Sound Practice	**B1** Word Endings	**C1** Rhyming Words	**D1** Buildups
sh<u>ow</u>	drop	<u>find</u>	m<u>a</u>ze
sl<u>ow</u>	dropped	<u>kind</u>	<u>a</u>maze
gr<u>ow</u>		m<u>ind</u>	amazing
<u>k</u>n<u>ow</u>	stop	**C2** Word Endings	**D2** Mixed Practice
A2 Shifty Words	stopped	<u>tired</u>	after
ar<u>ou</u>nd	swim	<u>jumped</u>	gather
gr<u>ou</u>nd	swimming	<u>splash</u>ed	cl<u>ea</u>n
f<u>ou</u>nd	<u>being</u>	<u>look</u>ed	ch<u>u</u>nk
	<u>carrying</u>		al<u>o</u>ng
	<u>crawl</u>ed		<u>a</u>way

4. TRICKY WORDS Have students read each row for accuracy, then fluency.

| service | there | some | wonderful | guard | 5 |
| very | surface | where | you | any | 10 |

5. MULTISYLLABIC WORDS Have students read the word by parts, tell how many syllables are in the word, then read the whole word.

Ⓐ	pud•dle	puddle	plen•ty	plenty
Ⓑ	hun•gry	hungry	sud•den•ly	suddenly
Ⓒ	im•por•tant	important	Al•ex•an•der	Alexander

6. DICTATION Say the word. Have students say the word, then finger count and say the sounds. Have students say each sound as they touch or write it.

A1 Buildups	**B1** Rhyming Words
<u>a</u>n d	c <u>a k e</u>
<u>s</u> a n d	t <u>a k e</u>
<u>th</u> <u>o u</u> s a n d	m <u>a k e</u>

31

PROCEDURES

1. First Reading

Mix group and individual turns, independent of your voice. Have students work toward an accuracy goal of 0–2 errors and practice any difficult words.

2. Second Reading, Timed Reading: Repeated Reading

- Once the group accuracy goal has been achieved, time individual students for 30 or 60 seconds while the other children track with their fingers and whisper read.

- Determine words correct per minute. Record student scores. Celebrate when students reach their goals!

Wow! [Nick], you met your goal. That was your best score ever. You get to read to the principal this week.

3. Partner Reading: Repeated Reading (Checkout Opportunity)

While students are doing Partner Reading, listen to individuals read the passage. Work on accuracy and fluency, as needed.

4. Homework: Repeated Reading

Have students read the story at home.

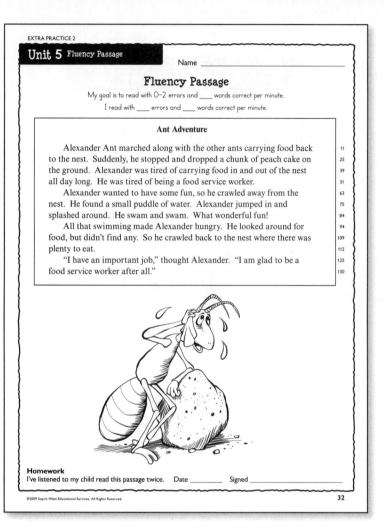

Unit 5 Fluency Passage

Name _____

Fluency Passage

My goal is to read with 0–2 errors and ____ words correct per minute.

I read with ____ errors and ____ words correct per minute.

Ant Adventure

Alexander Ant marched along with the other ants carrying food back to the nest. Suddenly, he stopped and dropped a chunk of peach cake on the ground. Alexander was tired of carrying food in and out of the nest all day long. He was tired of being a food service worker.

Alexander wanted to have some fun, so he crawled away from the nest. He found a small puddle of water. Alexander jumped in and splashed around. He swam and swam. What wonderful fun!

All that swimming made Alexander hungry. He looked around for food, but didn't find any. So he crawled back to the nest where there was plenty to eat.

"I have an important job," thought Alexander. "I am glad to be a food service worker after all."

	11
	25
	39
	51
	63
	75
	84
	94
	109
	112
	125
	130

Homework

I've listened to my child read this passage twice.   Date _____   Signed _____

32

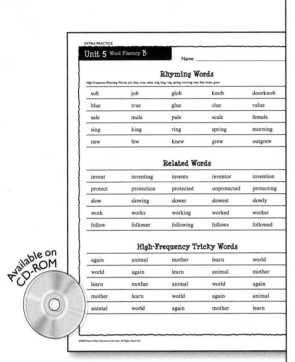

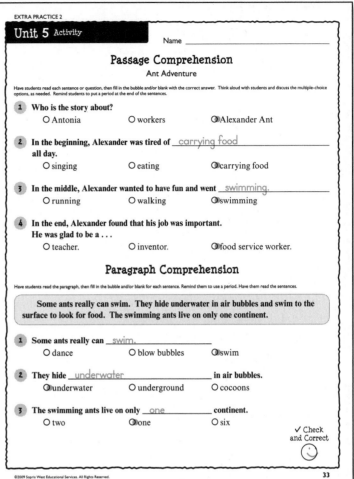

EXTRA PRACTICE 2

Unit 5 Activity

Name _____

Passage Comprehension
Ant Adventure

Have students read each sentence or question, then fill in the bubble and/or blank with the correct answer. Think aloud with students and discuss the multiple-choice options, as needed. Remind students to put a period at the end of the sentences.

1 Who is the story about?

○ Antonia   ○ workers   ◉ Alexander Ant

2 In the beginning, Alexander was tired of ___carrying food___ all day.

○ singing   ○ eating   ◉ carrying food

3 In the middle, Alexander wanted to have fun and went ___swimming.___

○ running   ○ walking   ◉ swimming

4 In the end, Alexander found that his job was important. He was glad to be a . . .

○ teacher.   ○ inventor.   ◉ food service worker.

Paragraph Comprehension

Have students read the paragraph, then fill in the bubble and/or blank for each sentence. Remind them to use a period. Have them read the sentences.

> Some ants really can swim. They hide underwater in air bubbles and swim to the surface to look for food. The swimming ants live on only one continent.

1 Some ants really can ___swim.___

○ dance   ○ blow bubbles   ◉ swim

2 They hide ___underwater___ in air bubbles.

◉ underwater   ○ underground   ○ cocoons

3 The swimming ants live on only ___one___ continent.

○ two   ◉ one   ○ six

✓ Check and Correct

©2009 Sopris West Educational Services. All Rights Reserved.   33

EXTRA PRACTICE

Unit 5 Word Fluency B

Name _____

Rhyming Words

High-Frequency Rhyming Words: job, blue, true, value, sing, king, ring, spring, morning, new, few, knew, grew

sob	job	glob	knob	doorknob
blue	true	glue	clue	value
sale	male	pale	scale	female
sing	king	ring	spring	morning
new	few	knew	grew	outgrew

Related Words

invent	inventing	invents	inventor	invention
protect	protection	protected	unprotected	protecting
slow	slowing	slower	slowest	slowly
work	works	working	worked	worker
follow	follower	following	follows	followed

High-Frequency Tricky Words

again	animal	mother	learn	world
world	again	learn	animal	mother
learn	mother	animal	world	again
mother	learn	world	again	animal
animal	world	again	mother	learn

©2009 Sopris West Educational Services. All Rights Reserved.

Available on CD-ROM

PROCEDURES

For each step, demonstrate and guide practice, as needed. Then have students complete the page independently.

1. Activity

Passage Comprehension

- Have students read each sentence or phrase, then fill in the bubble and/or blank with the correct answer.
- Think aloud with students and discuss the multiple-choice options, as needed.
- Remind students to put a period at the end of sentences.

Paragraph Comprehension

- Have students read the paragraph.
- Have students read each numbered sentence or phrase, then fill in the bubble and blank. Remind them to end sentences with a period, where needed.
- Have students read the completed sentences.

Self-monitoring

Have students read and check their work, then draw a happy face in the Check and Correct circle.

2. Word Fluency (BLMs are located on the CD.)

- To build fluency, have students read Rhyming Words, Related Words, and High-Frequency Tricky Words. Have students read each section three times in a row.
- To build accuracy, have students read all sets with partners.

> **ACCURACY BEFORE FLUENCY**
> **(Reminder)**
> Word Fluency is designed to build accuracy and fluency. Students should practice for accuracy before working on fluency.

PROCEDURES

1. **Sound Review**

   Use selected Sound Cards from Units 1–5.
   - Have students say each sound, building accuracy first, then fluency.
   - Mix group and individual turns, independent of your voice.

2. **Sounding Out Smoothly**
   - For each word, have students say the underlined part, sound out the word smoothly, then read the whole word. Use the words in sentences, as needed.
   - Have students read all the words in the row, building accuracy first, then fluency.
   - Repeat practice. Mix group and individual turns, independent of your voice.

3. **Accuracy and Fluency Building**
   - For each task, have students say any underlined part, then read each word.
   - Set a pace. Then have students read the whole words in each task and column.
   - Provide repeated practice, building accuracy first, then fluency.

4. **Tricky Words**

   Have students read each row for accuracy, then read the entire grid for fluency.

5. **Multisyllabic Words**

   For each word, have students read each syllable out loud, finger count the syllables, then tell how many syllables are in the word. If needed, use the word in a sentence. Have students read the whole word.

6. **Dictation**

   wait, white, might, long, song, strong
   - Say "wait." Have students say the word. Guide students as they finger count and say the sounds. Have students touch or write the sounds, then read the word. Say something like:

   The first word is *wait.* Say the word. (wait)
   Say and count the sounds in *wait* with me.

   Hold up one finger for each sound. /www/•/āāā/•/t/ How many sounds? (three)

   What's the first sound? (/www/) Touch under /www/.
   What's the next sound? (/āāā/) Write /āāā/ with the a-i pattern.
   What's the last sound? (/t/) Touch under /t/.
   Read the word. (wait)

   - Repeat with "white" and "might."
   - Continue with the rhyming words: long, song, strong.

EXTRA PRACTICE 3

Unit 5 Decoding Practice

Name _____

1. SOUND REVIEW Use selected Sound Cards from Units 1–5.

2. SOUNDING OUT SMOOTHLY Have students say the underlined part, sound out and read each word, then read the row.

<u>ea</u>ch	k<u>e</u>pt	qu<u>ee</u>n	<u>e</u>gg

3. ACCURACY/FLUENCY BUILDING Have students say any underlined part, then read each word. Next, have students read the column.

A1 Sound Practice	**B1** Word Endings	**C1** Compound Words	**D1** Buildups
<u>o</u>ver	<u>care</u>ful	inside	<u>art</u>
<u>o</u>pen	<u>use</u>ful	something	st<u>art</u>
	<u>wonder</u>ful	together	st<u>art</u>ed
gr<u>ow</u>		herself	
kn<u>ow</u>	<u>happen</u>ed		**D2** Sound Practice
	<u>happen</u>ing	**C2** Bossy E	<u>a</u>round
gr<u>ew</u>		l<u>i</u>ke	<u>a</u>dult
kn<u>ew</u>	thin	c<u>a</u>me	<u>a</u>maze
	thinner	s<u>a</u>fe	<u>a</u>mazing
Abb<u>y</u>		th<u>e</u>se	
bod<u>y</u>			
bab<u>y</u>			

4. TRICKY WORDS Have students read each row for accuracy, then fluency.

guard	other	animals	again	cocoon	5
change	changing	pushed	worm	warm	10

5. MULTISYLLABIC WORDS Have students read the word by parts, tell how many syllables are in the word, then read the whole word.

Ⓐ	thou•sands	thousands	nurs•ery	nursery
Ⓑ	nev•er	never	fin•al•ly	finally
Ⓒ	com•mu•ni•ties	communities	me•ta•mor•pho•sis	metamorphosis

6. DICTATION Say the word. Have students say the word, then finger count and say the sounds. Have students say each sound as they touch or write it.

A1 Shifty Words	**B1** Rhyming Words
w <u>ai</u> t	l <u>o n</u> g
wh <u>i</u> t e	s <u>o n</u> g
<u>m</u> igh t	st r <u>o n</u> g

34

PROCEDURES

1. First Reading

Mix group and individual turns, independent of your voice. Have students work toward an accuracy goal of 0–2 errors and practice any difficult words.

2. Second Reading, Short Passage Practice: Developing Prosody

- Demonstrate how to read a line or two with expression. Read at a rate slightly faster than the students' rate. Say something like:

  Listen as I read the first two sentences with expression and phrasing. I'm going to emphasize certain words and pause between sentences.

  "Abby Ant started out as an egg. She was round and white and smooth."

- Guide practice with your voice.
  Now read the paragraph with me.

- Provide individual turns while others track with their fingers and whisper read.
  Provide descriptive, positive feedback.
  [Manuel], you read with wonderful expression!

Unit 5 Fluency Passage

Name _____

Fluency Passage

My goal is to read with 0–2 errors and ____ words correct per minute.

I read with ____ errors and ____ words correct per minute.

Metamorphosis

Abby Ant started out as an egg. She was round and white and	13
smooth. The nursery workers kept her warm and safe. One day,	24
something odd happened. Her body got longer and thinner, and she	35
pushed herself out of the egg. She looked like a worm.	46
More changes kept happening. Her skin got tight, then fell off. This	58
happened over and over again. Abby never knew how she would look or	71
feel at the end of each day.	78
Next, Abby spun a cocoon around her body and hid for a long time.	92
But inside the cocoon, she kept changing.	99
One day, the nursery ants bit open her cocoon, and Abby came out.	112
Finally, Abby was an adult ant with three body parts and six legs.	125

Homework

I've listened to my child read this passage twice. Date _____ Signed _____

35

3. Partner Reading: Repeated Reading (Checkout Opportunity)

While students are doing Partner Reading, listen to individuals read the passage. Work on accuracy and fluency, as needed.

4. Homework: Repeated Reading

Have students read the story at home.

PROCEDURES

For each step, demonstrate and guide practice, as needed. Then have students complete the page independently.

1. Activity
Passage Comprehension

- Have students read each sentence or phrase, then fill in the bubble and/or blank with the correct answer.
- Think aloud with students and discuss the multiple-choice options, as needed.
- Remind students to put a period at the end of sentences.

Paragraph Comprehension

- Have students read the paragraph.
- Have students read each numbered sentence or phrase, then fill in or check the blank. Remind them to end sentences with a period, where needed.
- Have students read the completed sentences.

Self-monitoring

Have students read and check their work, then draw a happy face in the Check and Correct circle.

2. Word Fluency (BLMs are located on the CD.)

You may wish to have students repeat practice with Extra Practice, Word Fluency A or B.

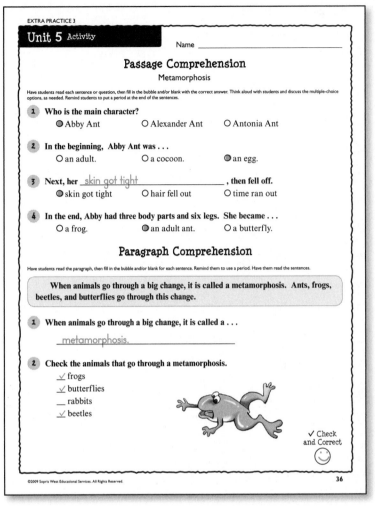

EXTRA PRACTICE 3

Unit 5 Activity

Name _____

Passage Comprehension
Metamorphosis

Have students read each sentence or question, then fill in the bubble and/or blank with the correct answer. Think aloud with students and discuss the multiple-choice options, as needed. Remind students to put a period at the end of the sentences.

1. Who is the main character?
   ● Abby Ant   ○ Alexander Ant   ○ Antonia Ant

2. In the beginning, Abby Ant was . . .
   ○ an adult.   ○ a cocoon.   ● an egg.

3. Next, her _skin got tight_____ , then fell off.
   ● skin got tight   ○ hair fell out   ○ time ran out

4. In the end, Abby had three body parts and six legs. She became . . .
   ○ a frog.   ● an adult ant.   ○ a butterfly.

Paragraph Comprehension

Have students read the paragraph, then fill in the bubble and/or blank for each sentence. Remind them to use a period. Have them read the sentences.

> When animals go through a big change, it is called a metamorphosis. Ants, frogs, beetles, and butterflies go through this change.

1. When animals go through a big change, it is called a . . .
   _metamorphosis._____

2. Check the animals that go through a metamorphosis.
   _✓_ frogs
   _✓_ butterflies
   ___ rabbits
   _✓_ beetles

✓ Check and Correct

36